This book is dedicated to Harriet Tubman, Eleanor Roosevelt, Babe Didrikson, Wilma Mankiller, Rosa Parks, Golda Meir, and others like them who, finding there were no paths, created them to make the journey easier for those of us who followed.

NICE GIRLS DON'T GET THE CORNER OFFICE

Unconscious Mistakes
Women Make
That Sabotage Their Careers

Lois P. Frankel

WARNER
BUSINESS
BOOKS™

NEW YORK   BOSTON

This publication is designed to provide competent and reliable information regarding the subject matter covered. However, it is sold with the understanding that the author and publisher are not engaged in rendering professional advice. If expert assistance is required, the services of a professional should be sought. The author and publisher specifically disclaim any liability that is incurred from the use or application of the contents of this book.

Copyright © 2004 by Lois P. Frankel, Ph.D.
All rights reserved.

Warner Business Books
Hachette Book Group USA
1271 Avenue of the Americas
New York, NY 10020

Visit our Web site at www.HachetteBookGroupUSA.com.

Printed in the United States of America

Originally published in hardcover by Warner Business Books, an imprint of Warner Books, Inc.

First International Trade Edition: December: 2004
10 9 8 7 6

Warner Business Books is a trademark of Time Warner Inc. or an affiliated company. Used under license by Hachette Book Group USA, which is not affiliated with Time Warner Inc.

ISBN: 0-446-69577-7

Book design and text composition by L&G McRee

Acknowledgments

Writing a book is a lot like giving a gift. I spend time choosing just the right words, wrap them in a package I think will delight you, and hope you'll enjoy reading them as much as I enjoyed writing them. It is only through the gifts of others that I can do this, and I want to share these people with you as I thank them, beginning with those who have graced my life the longest.

To the many friends, family, and associates around the world who believe in me, encourage me, share thoughts with me, and tolerate long periods of silence from me—thank you.

Everyone on the coaching team at Corporate Coaching International had a hand in this book, whether it be through support or actual contributions. I thank each of you, with a special acknowledgment to Dr. Pam Erhardt, Dr. Bruce Heller, Tom Henschel, and Susan Picascia, for so generously sharing your time and wisdom with me. You are not only colleagues but also dear friends.

Dr. Kim Finger, Tatum Barnett, and Majella Lue Sue—thank you not only for all your help with proofing and contributing ideas, but more importantly for giving me the gift of time to write. You ran CCI beautifully during my absences—I notice and appreciate it.

The many friends and clients of Corporate Coaching International—thank you for contributing anecdotes and examples of the mistakes women make that keep us from reaching our goals.

Bob Silverstein—finally, a literary agent I can trust! Thank you for so diligently representing me, coaching me, and offering your unique brand of friendship. Let's make more beautiful books together.

Diana Baroni and the staff at Warner Books—thank you for giving me the chance to write this book. I intend to keep the promise to take my act on the road and share this gift.

Contents

Introduction   *xiii*

Chapter 1   *Getting Started*   *1*

Chapter 2   *How You Play the Game*   *19*

1. Pretending It Isn't a Game   20
2. Playing the Game Safely and within Bounds   22
3. Working Hard   24
4. Doing the Work of Others   26
5. Working without a Break   28
6. Being Naive   30
7. Pinching Company Pennies   32
8. Waiting to Be *Given* What You Want   34
9. Avoiding Office Politics   38
10. Being the Conscience   40
11. Protecting Jerks   44
12. Holding Your Tongue   46
13. Failing to Capitalize on Relationships   48
14. Not Understanding the Needs of Your Constituents   50

Chapter 3   *How You Act*   *53*

15. Polling Before Making a Decision   54
16. Needing to Be Liked   56
17. Not Needing to Be Liked   58

18. Not Asking Questions for Fear of Sounding Stupid   60
19. Acting Like a Man   62
20. Telling the Whole Truth and Nothing but the Truth
    (So Help You God)   65
21. Sharing Too Much Personal Information   68
22. Being Overly Concerned with Offending Others   70
23. Denying the Importance of Money   72
24. Flirting   74
25. Acquiescing to Bullies   76
26. Decorating Your Office Like Your Living Room   78
27. Feeding Others   80
28. Offering a Limp Handshake   82
29. Being Financially Insecure   84
30. Helping   87

Chapter 4   *How You Think*   89

31. Making Miracles   90
32. Taking Full Responsibility   92
33. Obediently Following Instructions   94
34. Viewing Men in Authority as Father Figures   96
35. Limiting Your Possibilities   98
36. Ignoring the Quid Pro Quo   102
37. Skipping Meetings   104
38. Putting Work Ahead of Your Personal Life   106
39. Letting People Waste Your Time   108
40. Prematurely Abandoning Your Career Goals   110
41. Ignoring the Importance of Network Relationships   113
42. Refusing Perks   116
43. Making Up Negative Stories   118
44. Striving for Perfection   120

Chapter 5   *How You Brand and Market Yourself*   123

45. Failing to Define Your Brand   124
46. Minimizing Your Work or Position   126

47. Using Only Your Nickname or First Name   128
48. Waiting to Be Noticed   130
49. Refusing High-Profile Assignments   132
50. Being Modest   134
51. Staying in Your Safety Zone   136
52. Giving Away Your Ideas   138
53. Working in Stereotypical Roles or Departments   140
54. Ignoring Feedback   142
55. Being Invisible   144

Chapter 6   *How You Sound*   147

56. Couching Statements as Questions   148
57. Using Preambles   150
58. Explaining   152
59. Asking Permission   154
60. Apologizing   156
61. Using Minimizing Words   158
62. Using Qualifiers   160
63. Not Answering the Question   162
64. Talking Too Fast   164
65. The Inability to Speak the Language of Your Business   166
66. Using Nonwords   168
67. Using Touchy-Feely Language   170
68. The Sandwich   172
69. Speaking Softly   176
70. Speaking at a Higher-than-Natural Pitch   178
71. Trailing Voice Mails   180
72. Failing to Pause or Reflect Before Responding   182

Chapter 7   *How You Look*   185

73. Smiling Inappropriately   186
74. Taking Up Too Little Space   188
75. Using Gestures Inconsistent with Your Message   190

76. Being Over- or Underanimated   192

77. Tilting Your Head   194

78. Wearing Inappropriate Makeup   196

79. Wearing the Wrong Hairstyle   198

80. Dressing Inappropriately   200

81. Sitting on Your Foot   202

82. Grooming in Public   204

83. Sitting in Meetings with Your Hands under the Table   206

84. Wearing Your Reading Glasses around Your Neck   208

85. Accessorizing Too Much   210

86. Failing to Maintain Eye Contact   212

Chapter 8   *How You Respond*   *215*

87. Internalizing Messages   216

88. Believing Others Know More than You   219

89. Taking Notes, Getting Coffee, and Making Copies   222

90. Tolerating Inappropriate Behavior   224

91. Exhibiting Too Much Patience   228

92. Accepting Dead-End Assignments   230

93. Putting the Needs of Others Before Your Own   232

94. Denying Your Power   234

95. Allowing Yourself to Be the Scapegoat   237

96. Accepting the Fait Accompli   239

97. Permitting Others' Mistakes to Inconvenience You   242

98. Being the Last to Speak   244

99. Playing the Gender Card   246

100. Tolerating Sexual Harassment   249

101. Crying   251

Appendix   *Personal Development Planning and Resources*   *255*

Introduction

As an executive coach and corporate trainer, my success and reputation are dependent on people achieving their goals as a result of our work together. As one client said at the beginning of a coaching engagement, "I want this to be more than a fond memory. I want a promotion." Whether it's facilitating workshops at which women learn techniques for achieving their goals, coaching women one-on-one in these same areas, or having had a practice of psychotherapy devoted almost exclusively to workingwomen, I've worked with literally thousands of women. Add leadership workshops where both men and women were present, and we're talking about the opportunity to work with several thousand more people. This book is a composite of nearly twenty-five years' experience as a coach, trainer, human resource professional, and psychotherapist. It's about the unique mistakes I see women make at work, the coaching suggestions I provide to help them take charge of their careers, and the ways in which women hold themselves back from achieving their full potential.

The mistakes described in each chapter are real, as are the accompanying examples (although the identities have been altered to maintain confidentiality). The coaching tips at the end of each section are *identical* to the ones I provide to women around the world. Many of these women later report that the suggestions helped them get promoted, hired, a raise, more respect from their management and peers, or the confidence needed to start their own businesses. I measure my own effectiveness through *their* success stories.

But you should know from the outset—this book isn't for everyone. Many women have found ways to overcome the stereotypes they learned in childhood and act in empowered ways most of the time (it's nearly impossible to act empowered *all* the time). Whether it's by honing your own unique style of communication and behavior, or adopting and modifying more stereotypically masculine behaviors, you may be one of those women who is satisfied with the degree of professional success you've achieved. If that's you, you may find some additional tips in this book to help you further develop your unique style, but you've probably incorporated many of the coaching tips into your already successful repertoire. To you I say, "You go, girl!"

Other women may find they've tried to do the same only to find they're criticized by men and women alike for their strident or atypical behaviors. If you fall into this category, this book will seem the antithesis of all you've worked toward and, therefore, will be difficult for you to relate to. Not to worry, though. There are plenty of other books out there written just for you.

How do you know if this book will help *you?* Simple. First read through the following list of ten characteristics and check those that you can honestly say are typical of you most of the time:

_____ Most people describe me as professional.
_____ I have the reputation of being credible.
_____ I am known for being assertive.
_____ I have been told I am capable.
_____ When I speak, others get the idea I am intelligent.
_____ I am comfortable with being direct.
_____ My way of speaking causes others to describe me as articulate.
_____ I would say when it comes to the workplace, I am politically astute.

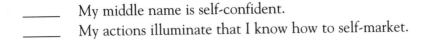

_____ My middle name is self-confident.
_____ My actions illuminate that I know how to self-market.

If you've checked all ten items, it's time for you to write your own book. On the other hand, if you checked only zero through seven items, this book was written with you in mind. Not only are these characteristics critical for success (for women *and* men), but I have also found that they are the development areas women most frequently address in their coaching engagements. The majority of women I coach don't have to work on all ten areas (although I've known a few who do), but rather identify two or three as requiring development if they are to achieve their career goals.

During the writing process, I happened to discuss some of the concepts included in the book with a client I'd been coaching for about six months. She said simply, "Why don't you just tell them what you tell me? *Quit bein' a girl.*" I had to smile. My words came back to haunt me. She was right. Those are the precise words I have told women of all ages and stages in their careers for more than two decades. I said those words to my clients when I had my practice of psychotherapy and I said them even more when I started my work as an executive coach. After all, nice *girls* don't get the corner office.

From therapy rooms to conference rooms, for nearly twenty-five years I have listened to women tell stories of how they were over-looked for promotions and placated when they expressed their ideas. I observed women in hundreds of meetings. The thread common to those who were ignored was how they acted in and reacted to their situations. I could hear and see the ways in which they unknowingly undermined their credibility and sabotaged their own careers. No one had to do it for them.

Knowing that women engage in self-defeating behaviors wasn't enough—I wanted to know *why*. Why would such smart, capable women act in ways detrimental to their career mobility (not to mention mental health)? During my career working with literally thousands of professional men and women, and comparing their behaviors, I found the answer to that question through inquiry and study. *From early childhood, girls are taught that their well-being and ultimate success is contingent upon acting in certain stereotypical ways, such as being polite, soft-spoken, compliant, and relationship-oriented.* Throughout their lifetimes, this is reinforced through media, family, and social messages. It's not that women *consciously* act in self-sabotaging ways; they simply act in ways consistent with their learning experiences.

Attempts to act counter to this socialized role are met with ridicule, disapproval, and scorn. Whether it was Mom's message—"Boys don't like girls who are too loud"—or, in response to an angry outburst, a spouse's message—"What's the matter? Is it that time of the month?"—women are continually bombarded with negative reinforcement for acting in any manner contrary to what they were taught in girlhood. As a result, they learn that acting like a "good girl" is less painful than assuming behaviors more appropriate for adult women (and totally acceptable for boys and adult men). In short, women wind up acting like girls, even after they're grown up. So when I told that client to "quit bein' a girl" the meta-message was, *You don't have to act in ways you were taught. You have choices. Grow into your role as a leader.*

Now, is this to say gender bias no longer exists in the workplace? Not at all. Women still earn only about 72 percent of the salaries earned by their male counterparts, must work twice as hard to be considered half as good as their male colleagues, and are more likely to be overlooked for promotions to senior levels of an organization. Research shows that on performance evaluation ratings, women consistently score less favorably than men. And *Fortune* magazine reports that only eleven of the one thousand largest companies in the country are headed by women. These are the realities. But after all these years I continue to go to the place of, "So what?"

We can rationalize, defend, and bemoan these facts, or we can acknowledge that these are the realities within which we must work. Rationalizing, defending, and bemoaning won't get us where we want to be. They become excuses for staying where we are.

I was trained at the University of Southern California as an existential clinician. It sounds fancy but all it really means is that it's the therapist's job to illuminate for the client the array of choices available. No matter what hand life deals us, we are ultimately left with the dilemma of how we choose to respond. That is where our control lies. It doesn't lie in the hand that's already been dealt. It doesn't lie in trying to change others—that's an illusion. It lies in the actions we choose to take in response to our situation. And when it comes to being women in the workplace, we can choose to behave in ways consistent with what others want and expect or we can choose another course—empowerment.

I am fully aware that there are those who say the term *empowerment* is outdated and overdone. I strongly disagree. The people who think it's overdone are those who possess the most power. Easy for them to say! They don't really want anyone to have the same power and influence that they enjoy, and so they downplay its importance in the employment and social arenas. It's a classic case of the desire to maintain the status quo. Those who have power don't really want to share it, so they minimize the need for others to share it. Without embarrassment or apology I say, *This book is about empowerment.*

Unlike other books that help you identify potential areas for development or point out critical success factors, this book doesn't stop there. Raising awareness is only the first step. Next, you need concrete suggestions for behavioral change that are *proven* to be effective in moving women forward in their careers. Behaviors that were appropriate in girlhood, but not in womanhood, may be contributing to your career's stagnating, plateauing, or even derailing from its career path. Success comes not from acting more like a man, as some might lead you to believe, but by acting more like a *woman* instead of a girl. Even if you select only 10 percent of the more than three hundred coaching tips provided in this book and incorporate them into your skill set, your investment will pay off.

How to Get the Most from This Book

The book contains 101 typical mistakes women make at work due to their socialization. Keep in mind most women don't make all 101 mistakes—but they do make more than one. I've found through my practice and experience that the more mistakes you make, the less likely you are to achieve your full career potential. I suggest you begin with the self-assessment in chapter 1. It will help you identify the self-defeating behaviors in which you most often engage.

After you've completed the self-assessment, you can go directly to those specific behaviors that get in your way most often. After each mistake, you will find tips for counteracting the mistake. As I said earlier, these are the same tips I give to my own clients when they come for coaching, so I know they work. But like a diet, they work only if you commit to them fully and apply them consistently.

In the space provided at the bottom of each page of coaching tips, check off the ones you commit to changing as a way of overcoming self-defeating behavior. Once you've finished the book, take these checked items and complete the personal development plan contained in the last chapter. Don't make it more complex than it needs to be. Choose just one behavior a week and focus on it. What you will find is that by focusing on it, you become increasingly aware of when and how you sabotage yourself. The next step is to replace the self-defeating behavior with more effective ones. You *can* do it. It's *your* choice. All it takes is acting more like the woman you are capable of becoming than like the girl you were taught to be.

Chapter 1

Getting Started

Here's your first coaching tip: *Don't begin reading this book until you've learned how to use it to your advantage.* You'll only end up thinking everything applies to you in equal proportions when in fact you're probably doing better than you think. You know how we women can be—more critical of ourselves than necessary and reluctant to take credit where it's due. When I coach women, I often tell them that changing behavior is much easier if they can understand where it comes from and what purpose it serves. All behavior serves a purpose—take a few minutes now to understand what purpose *yours* serves.

From the outset I want you to know and, even more important, believe that *the mistakes impeding you from reaching your career goals or potential don't happen because you're stupid or incompetent* (although others might want to make you think so). You are simply acting in ways consistent with your socialization. Beyond girlhood, no one ever *tells* us that acting differently is an option—and so we don't. Whether it's because we are discouraged from doing so or because we are unaware of the alternatives, we often fail to develop a repertoire of woman-appropriate behaviors.

As an executive coach to both men and women in organizations of all sizes around the world, I've had the opportunity to gain insight into why some people move forward fluidly in their careers while others stagnate, never fully reaching their potential. Although there are plenty of mistakes made by both men and women that hold them back, there are a unique set of mistakes made predominantly by women. Whether I'm working in Jakarta, Oslo, Prague, Frankfurt, Wellington, or Detroit, I'm amazed to watch women across cultures make the same mistakes at work. They may be more exaggerated in Hong Kong than in Houston, but they're variations on the same theme. And I know they're mistakes because once women address them and begin to act differently, their career paths take wonderful turns they never thought possible.

So why *do* women stay in the place of girlhood long after it's productive for them? One reason is because we've been taught that acting like a girl—even when we're grown up—isn't such a bad thing. Girls get taken care of in ways boys don't. Girls aren't expected to fend for or take care of themselves—others do that for them. Sugar and spice and everything nice—that's what little girls are made of. Who doesn't want to be everything nice?

The virtues of girls are extolled in songs. "I Enjoy Being a Girl." "Thank Heaven for Little Girls." "My Girl." "The Girl from Ipanema." Who *wouldn't* want to be a girl? People like girls. Men want to protect you. Cuddly or sweet, tall or tan, girls don't ask for much. They're nice to be around and they're nice to have around—sort of like pets.

Being a girl is certainly easier than being a woman. Girls don't have to take responsibility for their destiny. Their choices are limited by a narrowly defined scope of expectations. And here's another reason why we continue to exhibit the behaviors learned in childhood even when at some level we know they're holding us back: We can't see beyond the boundaries that have traditionally circumscribed the parameters of our influence. It's dangerous to go out of bounds. When you do, you get accused of trying to act like a man or being "bitchy." All in all, it's easier to behave in socially acceptable ways.

There's only one problem. When we live a life circumscribed by the expectations of others, we live a limited life. What does it really mean to live our lives as girls rather than women? It means we choose behaviors consistent with those that are expected of us rather than those that move us toward fulfillment and self-actualization. Rather than live consciously, we live reactively. Although we mature physically, we never really mature emotionally. And while this may allow us momentary relief from real-world dilemmas, it never allows us to be fully in control of our destiny.

As I said in the introduction, observing, coaching, and facilitating workshops for professional women have enabled me to learn firsthand how acting like a girl gets in the way of achieving your career potential. Missed opportunities for career-furthering assignments or promotions arise from being reluctant to showcase your capabilities, feeling hesitant to speak in meetings, and working so hard that you forget to build the relationships necessary for long-term success. These behaviors are only magnified in workshops at which men *and* women are the participants. My work in corporations allows me to facilitate both workshops for only women and leadership development programs for mixed groups within the same company. Even women whom I've seen act assertively in a group of other women become more passive, compliant, and reticent to speak in a mixed group.

The Case of Susan

Let me give you an example of a woman with whom I worked who wondered why she wasn't reaching her full potential. Susan was a procurement manager for a *Fortune* 100 oil company. She'd been with this firm for more than twelve years when she expressed frustration over not moving as far or as fast as male colleagues who'd commenced employment at the same time she did. Although Susan thought there might be gender bias at play, she never considered how she contributed to her own career plateauing. Before

Susan and I met one-on-one in a coaching session, I had the opportunity to observe her in meetings with her peers.

At the first meeting I noticed this attractive woman with long blond hair, diminutive figure, and deep blue eyes. Being from Texas, she spoke with a delicate Southern accent and had an alluring way of cocking her head and smiling as she listened to others. She was a pleasure to have in the room, but she reminded me of a cheerleader—attractive, vivacious, warm, and supportive. As others spoke, she nodded her head and smiled. When she did speak, she used equivocating phrases like "Perhaps we should consider . . ."; "Maybe it's because . . ."; and "What if we . . ." Because of these behaviors no one would ever accuse Susan of being offensive, but neither would they consider her executive material.

After several more meetings at which I observed her behavior vis-à-vis her peers, Susan and I met privately to explore her career aspirations. Based on her looks, demeanor, and what I had heard her say in meetings, I assumed she was perhaps thirty to thirty-five years old. I was floored when she told me she was forty-seven, with nearly twenty years' experience in the area of procurement. I had no clue she had that kind of history and experience—and if *I* didn't, no one else did either. Without realizing it, Susan was acting in ways consistent with her socialization. She had received so much positive reinforcement for these behaviors that she'd come to believe they were the only ways she could act and still be successful. Susan bought into the stereotype of bein' a girl.

Truth be told, the behaviors she exhibited in meetings did contribute to her early career success. The problem was that they would not contribute to reaching future goals and aspirations. Her management, peers, and direct reports acknowledged she was a delight to work with, but they didn't seriously consider her for more senior positions or high-visibility projects. Susan acted like a girl and, accordingly, was treated like one. Although she knew she had to do some things differently if she were to have any chance of reaching her potential, she didn't have a clue what they would be.

I eventually came to learn Susan was the youngest of four children and the only girl in the family. She was the apple of Daddy's eye and protected by her brothers. She learned early on that being a girl was a good thing. She used it to her advantage. And as Susan grew up, she continued to rely on the stereotypically feminine behaviors that resulted in getting her needs met. She was the student teachers loved having in class, the classmate with whom everyone wanted to be friends, and the cheerleader everyone admired. Susan had no reference for alternative ways of acting that would bring her closer to her dream of being promoted to a vice president position.

We're All Girls at Heart

Although Susan is an extreme example of how being a girl can pay huge dividends, most of us have some Susan in us. We behave in ways consistent with the roles we were socialized to play, thereby never completely moving from girlhood to womanhood. As nurturers, supporters, or helpmates, we are more invested in seeing others get their needs met than we are in ensuring that ours are acknowledged. And there's another catch. When we *do* try to break out of those roles and act in more mature, self-actualizing ways, we are often met with subtle—and not-so-subtle—resistance designed to keep us in a girl role. Comments like "You're so cute when you're angry," "What's the matter? Are you on the rag?" or "Why can't you be satisfied with where you are?" are designed to keep us in the role of a girl.

When others question our femininity or the validity of our feelings, our typical response is to back off rather than make waves. We question the veracity of our experience. If it's fight or flight, we often flee. And every time we do, we take a step back into girlhood and question our self-worth. In this way we collude with others to remain girls rather than become women. And here is where we must begin to accept responsibility for not getting our needs met or never reaching our full potential. Eleanor Roosevelt was right when she said, "No one can make you feel inferior without your consent." Stop consenting. Stop colluding. *Quit bein' a girl!*

Self-Assessment

Now it's time to assess where you need the most work. The inventory on the next few pages is designed to help you identify the specific behaviors that may impede your career movement. You'll find there are areas you've already worked to address and that no longer present obstacles to you. If you're like most women, you'll also find a few areas that still require your attention. Take time now to complete the inventory. When you're finished, there are some guidelines for how to apply your score to what you read. You may not even need to read the entire book. Imagine that! Your first lesson in working smarter, not harder.

CHART 1

SELF-ASSESSMENT

Using the scale below, decide how true each of the following statements is of you. Be as honest as possible, considering how you act, think, or feel most of the time or in most situations.

1= Rarely true
2= Sometimes true
3= Almost always true

2 1. I have no problem bending the rules if it will justify results.

1 2. It doesn't bother me if someone doesn't like me despite my best efforts to build a relationship.

1 3. I set realistic goals for how much I can reasonably accomplish in a day.

2 4. I can tell you in thirty seconds or less how I bring value to my firm.

1 5. When I give a serious message, I don't use a smile to soften it.

2 6. When I have an opinion, I say it directly rather than couch it as a question.

1 7. I recognize putdowns and let it be known I don't appreciate them.

2 8. I don't accept blame or responsibility for mistakes made by other people.

1 9. I'm not one to apologize for low-impact mistakes.

1 10. When given an unreasonable deadline, I negotiate for something more realistic.

_1_ 11. If someone fails to notice something I've done exceptionally well, I call attention to it myself.

_3_ 12. When sitting at a conference table, I put my elbows on the table and lean in.

_2_ 13. I'm comfortable with silence.

_3_ 14. I believe I'm as smart as the next person.

_1_ 15. I stand up for what I believe in, even if I know it will make others uncomfortable or unhappy.

_1_ 16. I am hesitant to share too much personal information at work.

_2_ 17. I plan how I will approach a task before jumping in.

_3_ 18. I actively seek new assignments that will stretch my talents.

_2_ 19. I've selected a hairstyle that is appropriate for my age and position.

_1_ 20. My verbal messages are crisp and concise.

_2_ 21. If I'm asked to take notes at more than one meeting, I tactfully decline to do so.

_1_ 22. I don't feel guilty when my own priorities make it impossible for me to do someone a favor.

_1_ 23. I don't take it personally if someone is offended by something I've said.

_0_ 24. I ask favors from people to whom I have given special assistance or attention.

_3_ 25. I volunteer for assignments that will profile my capabilities with senior management.

_2_ 26. I take care to wear accessories that complement my clothing.

_3_ 27. My voice is loud and clear.

_1_ 28. If someone treats me inappropriately, I let the person know how I feel about it.

_2_ 29. I consciously spend time each day engaging in casual conversations with colleagues.

_2_ 30. I have no problem asking for a raise if I think I deserve it.

_3_ 31. Regardless of how busy I am, I attend meetings at which I know I can showcase my skills.

_1_ 32. At least every other month, I ask others for feedback.

_1_ 33. I dress for the job I want, not the one I have.

_1_ 34. I don't use qualifiers (*sort of*, *kind of*, and the like).

_3_ 35. I'm among the first to speak at meetings.

_2_ 36. If I don't quite trust what someone is saying, I will ask questions to help assess if it's true.

_3_ 37. I offer a firm handshake that conveys the message that I am to be taken seriously.

_1_ 38. I don't cancel previously scheduled personal plans because of work.

_2_ 39. If someone repeats an idea I previously expressed, I tactfully call attention to where it originated.

_3_ 40. I don't apply lipstick or comb my hair in public.

_1_ 41. I speak slowly, taking all the time I need to express myself thoroughly.

_2_ 42. I advocate well for myself.

_1_ 43. I don't ask permission to spend company money for things I know are appropriate.

_1_ 44. My workspace is neat and well organized.

_1_ 45. I don't allow others to waste my time at work.

_1_ 46. When I'm acknowledged for a job well done, I let my boss know about it.

_3_ 47. I look people directly in the eye on first meeting them.

_1_ 48. I know what *ROI* means.

_2_ 49. I know I'm good at what I do.

CHART 2

SELF-ASSESSMENT SCORE SHEET

Step 1. Record your responses from the questionnaire in the spaces below.
Step 2. Add your scores down by column for a *category* score.
Step 3. Add your scores on the bottom line across for a *total* score.

1. Play	2. Act	3. Think	4. Market	5. Look	6. Sound	7. Respond	
1. 2	2. 1	3. 1	4. 2	5. 1	6. 2	7. 1	10
8. 2	9. 1	10. 1	11. 1	12. 3	13. 2	14. 3	13
15. 1	16. 1	17. 2	18. 3	19. 2	20. 1	21. 2	12
22. 1	23. 1	24. 1	25. 3	26. 2	27. 3	28. 1	12
29. 2	30. 2	31. 3	32. 1	33. 1	34. 1	35. 3	13
36. 2	37. 3	38. 1	39. 2	40. 3	41. 1	42. 2	14
43. 1	44. 1	45. 1	46. 1	47. 3	48. 1	49. 2	10
1. Play	2. Act	3. Think	4. Market	5. Look	6. Sound	7. Respond	TOTAL SCORE
11	10	10	13	15	11	14	84

21   31   44   59   70   84

INTERPRETATION

Circle your two highest scores on the bottom line. These are the two areas in which you are most comfortable acting in ways that contribute to your success in a positive, confident, and competent manner. They are your greatest strengths when it comes to achieving your career goals, so continue to exhibit these behaviors regardless of how much others may want you to minimize them.

Circle your two lowest scores on the bottom line. These are the two areas in which you have the most difficulty breaking free from stereotypically feminine behaviors. You may want to go straight to the corresponding chapters to read more about how you can complement your strengths with more of these behaviors.

If your total score is:

49–87	You've been socialized well, and it's probably not helping you to achieve your career goals. Pay close attention to those questions on which you rated yourself a 1—you're dangerously close to sabotaging your career.
88–127	You could do with a little fine-tuning. Focus on those areas where you still have difficulty with acting in stereotypical ways. You'll find that small changes pay big dividends.
128–149	You're doing a great job of countering the behaviors you learned in girlhood that could sabotage your career. Keep up the good work—no doubt it's paying off.

Unconscious Competence

See? I told you your behavior wasn't as bad as you thought. There's a model used in coaching for helping people develop new behaviors. It's called *Unconscious Competence*. The following chart illustrates how it works.

CHART 3

UNCONSCIOUS COMPETENCE

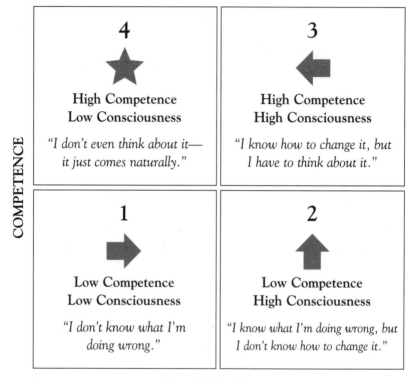

CONSCIOUSNESS

Your challenge is to move from Box 1 to Box 4 *over a period of time*. You begin in Box 1—unaware that you're even doing anything wrong, so you can't possibly have competence in that area (low consciousness and low competence).

After taking the self-assessment and reading the mistakes described in this book, you'll be more aware of your self-defeating behaviors, but you still won't know what to do to change them. You've moved to Box 2—still low competence but now high consciousness.

By actually practicing the coaching tips contained after each mistake, you'll move to Box 3—high consciousness and high competence. If you've ever learned to play a sport or musical instrument, you're familiar with how this works. You'll become increasingly capable of incorporating these behaviors into your regular repertoire of skills, not even thinking about when you do them (Box 4—high competence and low consciousness). Although this is the goal, don't be discouraged if in some cases it doesn't come naturally. Whether it's a golf swing or a piano piece, you know you can do it but you may have to concentrate on doing it well. That's Box 3.

As when you're learning to acquire any new skill, for a while you'll be self-conscious about how you're acting. Finally, after a period of practice and success, you'll incorporate these behaviors without thinking. In some areas, however, you may never quite get there. Socialization can make it difficult—no, change that to *impossible*—to engage in certain behaviors without having to think about it first. There's nothing wrong with this. As long as you act consciously and purposefully, you'll be fine.

Managing Your Anxiety

I can see by the looks on women's faces, and from their comments, that anxiety and confusion are part of the learning process. My 1989 audiotape, *Women and Power: Understand Your Fear/Releasing Your Potential,* and my book, *Women, Anger & Depression: Strategies for Self-Empowerment* (Health Communications, 1991) contain now dated examples, but the content related to the process remains on target. More than a decade later, when the suggestion is made to embrace their power, women reject the notion of being perceived as too masculine, aggressive, or uncooperative out of fear. It is so counter to our socialization that we dismiss it out of hand. The notion that we must be for others rather than for ourselves is implanted so strongly that we are reluctant to explore the alternative.

The irony is that women act powerfully all the time, but in ways different from men. Relying on our "girlish charm" can be just as influential, but less direct and less confrontational. In other words, we wield power less directly than men. We've learned to be less direct so we will not be perceived as taking too much power away from men. This is at the core of our difficulties with gaining increased influence skills and organizational visibility.

Each time a woman *directly* asserts herself, however, she is essentially saying to the men in her life (whether they are husbands, sons, bosses, or other male authority figures), "I want something from you. I want what is rightfully mine. I expect my needs to be met, too." With each assertion we frequently feel guilty. We equate taking control *back* with taking something *away* from someone else. More than simply getting what we need, deserve, or want, we are forcing others to give back what we have been giving away for so long. The reactions we get are difficult to cope with. Others don't really want the situation to change—*they* already have everything *they* need, so why should they change?

Resistance to change is normal. It is to be expected. Like the alcoholic in recovery who finds others colluding to bring him or her back to a place of intoxication, the girl who moves toward womanhood will find herself faced with people who want to continue to infantilize her. This is what you must keep in mind if you want to achieve your goals.

What's a Girl to Do?

Here are some specific coaching tips—a prelude of what is to follow. Take them one at a time. Don't try to do them all at once—you'll only set yourself up for frustration. Choose one or two on which to work, then come back for more.

• **Give yourself permission to move from girlhood to womanhood.** It may seem like a simple idea, but it's one that is often resisted for all the reasons mentioned above. Have a good, long talk with yourself. Tell yourself that you are not only allowed, but *entitled* to act in ways that move you toward goal attainment. Try the mantra *I am entitled to have my needs met, too*.

• **Visualize yourself as you want to be.** If you can see it, you can have it. Picture yourself in the role to which you aspire. If it's in the corner office, see yourself at the desk with the accoutrements that go along with it. Consider the behaviors in which you will engage to warrant this position and the ways in which you will act. Bring them into your reality.

• **Talk back to the fearful voice inside your head.** This may sound crazy at first, but you must counter the old messages and replace them with new ones. If your fearful girl's voice says, "But no one will like me if I change," let your woman's voice respond with, "That's an old message. Let's create a new, more empowered one."

• **Surround yourself with a Plexiglas shield.** The Plexiglas shield is designed to allow you to see what is going on around you, but not be punctured by the negativity of others. I suggested this to a client, who later told me she thought it sounded a little crazy but decided to try it—only to find that it worked! In difficult situations she would picture herself encapsulated in a Plexiglas bubble that protected her from the disparaging remarks of others and allowed her to remain in a grounded, adult position.

- **Create the word on the street.** A routine exercise we do in leadership classes is to ask participants to write a twenty-five-word vision statement of how they want to be described, then list the behaviors needed to get them there. You can do the same. Write down what you want others to be saying about you, then follow it up with specific actions to make it happen. In short, accept the responsibility of adulthood.

- **Recognize resistance and put a name to it.** When you find others resisting your efforts to be more direct and empowered, consider first that their responses are designed to keep you in a less powerful place. Rather than acquiesce, question it. Say something like, "It seems you don't agree with what I'm saying. Let me give you the rationale for my position and then perhaps you can tell me what it is you take issue with."

- **Ask for feedback.** If you're worried that you are in some way acting inappropriately, ask a trusted friend or colleague for feedback. Avoid asking a yes–no question (such as, "Did you think I was out of line?"). Try asking an open-ended question that will give you insight into how you are perceived (such as, "Tell me what I did in that meeting that helped me or hindered me from achieving my goals").

- **Don't aim for perfection.** Even *I* don't engage in all the behaviors described in this book. There are some that are just so counter to my personality, I don't even try; others that, no matter how hard I try, I don't do well. The important thing is to do a few really well and allow the rest to fall into place.

Next Steps

You'll be on your own in just a minute. I suggest you begin by reading the two chapters that coincide with your *lowest* scores. This is where you need the most help. Not every mistake in those chapters will apply to you, so don't get carried away and make every coaching tip a goal. Instead, check the box at the bottom of the page of those tips you think will make the biggest difference and commit to taking action on those. Avoid the tendency to ignore the tips that seem hard. That's probably where you can get the greatest leverage in changes to your behavior.

After you've read the sections that correspond with your lowest scores, go back and review the remaining mistakes. All 101 mistakes are real mistakes made by real women. They were accumulated as the result of my own work as a coach, soliciting input from men and women in companies I've worked with around the world, and contributions made from women who attended my Quit Bein' a Girl workshops. Women who heard through friends that I was writing this book even sent unsolicited e-mails and were eager to share their mistakes with you.

As for the coaching tips, most of them are ones I've provided to women for years and gotten feedback that even small changes have a big impact on how they are perceived. Others were provided by my colleagues on the consulting team at Corporate Coaching International who are subject-matter experts in various coaching areas such as communications, strategic career planning, and work–life balance. As you read the tips, you'll find I make reference to books or classes. The very last chapter provides you with two important things: a summary of these references, with contact information, and a personal development plan template. If you're serious about achieving your personal and professional best, I urge you to complete the plan soon after reading the book. It will help to keep you on track and allow you to chart your own progress. Now it's up to you. Go get 'em!

Chapter 2

How You Play the Game

Many women—especially those of us who grew up in the 1950s and 1960s—never had the opportunity to participate in competitive sports. Until just recently, few of us served in the armed forces, attended military academies, or participated in other activities that required us to play to win. As a result, we don't know how to play the game, let alone play within bounds but at the edge (which will be explored further a little later in this chapter). Worse yet, many women view the whole idea of the game of business as something unpleasant, dirty, and to be avoided at all costs.

Let's start with the most important lesson: Business *is* a game and you *can* win it. As a matter of fact, women are born to win this game. I spend half of my time working with men, teaching them to be more like women. Of course, I don't put it quite that way or I would be out of business. Instead, I talk to them about the importance of things like listening, collaborating, motivating, and seeing the human side of their staff. These are typically things women do well because they've been taught the behaviors and have had a lot of practice at them.

The areas in which women often aren't quite as skilled as men are knowing where the imaginary boundaries are and understanding the unspoken rules. Of all the coaching tips in this book, the following ones are the most difficult for women to incorporate into their corporate skill set. Many of the suggestions are counter to everything we learned growing up. Resist the urge to skip the hard stuff. If you don't play, you can't win.

Mistake 1

Pretending It Isn't a Game

$\mathcal{T}$he workplace is exactly that—a game. It has rules, boundaries, winners, *and* losers. Women tend to approach work more like an event (picnic, concert, fund-raiser) where everyone comes together for the day to play together nicely. In our desire to create win–win situations, we unknowingly create win–lose ones—where *we're* the losers. Playing the game of business doesn't mean you're out to cause others to fail, but it is competitive. It means you are aware of the rules and develop strategies for making them work to your advantage.

Barbara is an example of someone who didn't understand the game. She worked as the director of marketing in the banking industry for many years. She reached the point in her career where she was so successful that she was sought after for senior positions by a number of companies. She selected one, in the specialty chemicals business, where she entered as a vice president. When she was referred to me for coaching, she could not understand why she was foundering. Everything that had worked for her in banking, failed her in her new position. Her polite, laid-back way of managing and interacting with others was now seen as weak and indecisive. Not understanding that this was a new ball game, Barbara played the new game by the old rules—and found herself facing the possibility of failure for the first time in her career.

Not only is business a game, but the rules of the game change from organization to organization and from department to department *within* an organization. What works with one boss may not work with the next one. Keeping your eye on the ball is essential when it comes to winning the game of business.

COACHING TIPS

- Learn to play chess. It will help you develop a more strategic mind.
- Make a list of the rules of the game at your workplace. Remember, these are usually unspoken expectations for how fast-trackers should behave. You may not be able to do the entire list at one time, but rather may have to observe interactions, memos, and meetings in a different way than you have in the past. Examples of rules in some workplaces include *Don't disagree with the boss, Everyone works at least ten hours of overtime, Being polite is more important than being right, Deadlines must be met no matter what the circumstance, Budgets are strictly adhered to, The customer always comes first,* and so on. As you make your list, begin thinking about how your behavior compares with the expectations.
- Read *Hardball for Women: Winning at the Game of Business* by Pat Heim, Ph.D. It will help you better understand the male business culture and how to use it to your advantage. Among the tips provided are ways to be assertive without being obnoxious, how to engage in smart self-promotion, and methods to display confidence even when you may feel powerless.
- Identify a mentor—someone who is successful at playing the game and with whom you can openly discuss the rules in your organization.
- If you don't currently play a sport—start. It doesn't matter whether it's tennis, softball, or golf. Playing sports helps you learn the language of the game.

ACTION ITEM

Mistake 2

Playing the Game Safely and within Bounds

$\mathcal{A}$s an avid but quite average tennis player, I used to hit the ball squarely within bounds for fear of going out and losing the point. In an effort to play safely, I artificially narrowed my playing field. After a while, it occurred to me that I would never win the game playing that way. I had to learn to hit the ball toward the edges of, yet within, bounds if I ever hoped to win. So I started going outside my comfort zone and found that I actually won more games.

I had the opportunity to use this analogy with a client who was recently promoted to supervisor and getting feedback she wasn't "proactive" enough. "How can I be accused of not being proactive?" she wondered. "I do everything I'm supposed to without being asked." Doing everything you're supposed to isn't proactive. It's only doing what you're supposed to. At her new level, management expected her to take more responsibility and make decisions independently. When I suggested this to her, she said she didn't want to overstep her authority, so she ran most important decisions by her supervisor first.

I asked the woman if she played tennis and, fortunately, she did. Within moments of using the analogy of playing it safe in tennis, she got it. She could understand how she wasn't using all the court available to her. By making assumptions about what would and wouldn't be acceptable to her management, she narrowed her playing field. Rather than risking hitting the ball out of bounds, she only engaged in behaviors she knew would land the ball squarely within the court. It wasn't enough for the woman's manager, who wanted her team members to take calculated risks and go beyond what was asked of them.

This same phenomenon plays out in the workplace all the time.

Even when a woman knows the workplace is a game, she has the tendency to play safe rather than play smart. She obeys all the rules to the letter and expects others to as well. If the policy says don't do it, then it can't be done. If it might upset someone, she doesn't do it. You never want to act unethically, but it *is* a game—and one you want to win. To do so you have to use the entire field available to you.

In my client's case, she followed my suggestion to ask her manager to help her define her scope of authority so that she would feel more comfortable taking risks. The manager called me several weeks later and, during the course of conversation about another matter, mentioned that the woman was now showing more initiative and meeting her performance objectives.

COACHING TIPS

- Play the game within bounds, but at the edges.
- Write down two rules you interpret narrowly and always follow. Have you seen other people bend these rules? If so, what's happened to them? If nothing, then take the risk of stretching the bounds by broadly, rather than narrowly, interpreting the rules.
- If you're not sure something is *fair*, do it anyway. If you're not sure something is *ethical*, ask.
- If you're called out, don't take it personally—and by all means don't revert to playing safe. Look at it as an opportunity to learn where the edge of the boundary is and how to play to it.

ACTION ITEM

Mistake 3

Working Hard

*T*here's a popular saying: *Women have to work twice as hard to be considered half as good.* As a result, women are like little ants— working, working, working. They complain that they do more than everyone else, and they do! It's a myth that people get ahead because they work hard. The truth is, no one ever got promoted purely because of hard work. Likability, strategic thinking, net-working, being a team player are but a few of the other factors that go into crafting a successful career.

Everyone is expected to carry his or her fair share of the weight. This doesn't mean you should focus exclusively on working hard. Sometimes I think women do so because it's easier to do what we know best, rather than to engage in behaviors that seem foreign to you. One woman complained to me about the guys she worked with who, every Monday morning during football season, spent the first half hour of the day rehashing Sunday's games with the boss.

"What a waste of time. Here I am working away and they're talking about football!" she lamented. What bothered her even more was the fact these same guys were being tapped for prime assignments. Whereas women see it as "wasting the company's money" to do anything other than focus on the task at hand between 8 A.M. and 5 P.M., men know that whether it's talking about football or last weekend's golf scores, they're building rela-tionships that will later work for them. In this situation her male coworkers were bonding with the boss in a way that allowed him to better know these team members. As a result, when growth oppor-tunities became available, he picked them because he was familiar and comfortable with them.

And herein lies one of business's best-kept secrets. People aren't hired and promoted simply because they work hard. It happens because the decision maker knows the *character* of the person and feels confident about his or her ability not only to do the job, but also to do it in a way that promotes collegial team relationships. By keeping her nose to the grindstone, the woman was actually acting in a way detrimental to getting what she most wanted—more interesting work and an opportunity to show she was capable of doing more.

COACHING TIPS

- Give yourself permission to "waste" a little time. If you're not spending 5 percent of your day building relationships, you're doing something wrong.
- Define your work hours and stick with them. Remember Parkinson's Law—*Work expands to fill the time available*. This isn't to say there won't be times when you must work overtime, but if you're consistently the last one left at the office, there's something wrong with that picture.
- At the beginning of each day, define what you want to accomplish. You can avoid the tendency to take on whatever comes across your desk during the course of the day by deliberately scheduling it for a later time.

ACTION ITEM

Mistake 4

Doing the Work of Others

*W*hen Harry S. Truman said, "The buck stops here," surely he was thinking of a woman. Our tendency to take responsibility for not only our own work but also the work of others is yet another self-defeating behavior. Yes, you have a responsibility to your employer to ensure the delivery of a high-quality product or service, but it is not your responsibility *alone*. Women have a nasty habit of saying, "Well, if I don't do it, no one else will." This only ensures that *you'll* be doing it—and for a l-o-n-g time.

And there's another problem associated with taking too much responsibility. While women are doing the grunt work, men are building their careers. They're no fools. Promotions are rewards for getting the job done, not necessarily doing the job. I had a boss once who told me there are two kinds of people in the world: careerists and achievers. Achievers keep busy by doing the work. Careerists spend their time managing their careers. Truth be known, you've got to be a little of both to get ahead.

COACHING TIPS

- Stop volunteering for low-profile, low-impact assignments. If necessary, sit on your hand rather than raise it.
- Recognize when people delegate inappropriately to you. Practice saying unapologetically, "You know, I'd love to help you out with this but I'm just swamped." Then stop talking. Avoid the inclination to want to solve the problem for them. It's *their* problem, not yours.
- If you're a manager or supervisor, don't let people delegate up. This most often happens when people reporting to you claim to be unable to perform a task or say they don't have the time. Avoid the tendency to take it over because it will be faster if you do it yourself. Instead, suggest they ask a coworker for technical assistance or, if you have the time, use it as a teaching opportunity.
- Use self-talk to replace feeling guilty about saying no. Try saying something like, "I don't have to feel guilty about seeing that my needs are met."

ACTION ITEM

Mistake 5

Working without a Break

*T*here's certainly truth to the adage, *If you need something done, give it to a woman.* Women will work *nonstop* to crank out a project. Working without a break not only is damaging to your health, but actually impedes optimum performance as well. Productivity experts suggest that a break every ninety minutes is required to maintain maximum levels of concentration and accuracy.

Working without a break also contributes to the impression that you're flustered or inefficient. One executive told me a female vice president reporting to him made him feel "uncomfortable" because she always looked like she was overworked and harried (a word you *rarely* hear used to describe a man). Working through lunch hours or without coming up for air won't get you ahead. Giving the impression you are always up to your ears in alligators could hinder being given special projects or assignments that could later bring you recognition.

COACHING TIPS

- Get in the habit of getting up from your desk for a stretch break at least once every ninety minutes.
- At the beginning of each week, make it a point to schedule at least one lunch meeting.
- Schedule times throughout the day to drop by a colleague's office for a few minutes of casual conversation. When someone drops by yours, stop what you're doing and invite him or her in.
- Use the alarm function on your computer to remind you of your break (and when it goes off . . . take your break).
- Use the lunch hour to your advantage. Join a Toastmasters club, run an errand that will allow you to get home earlier after work, or just take a walk and refresh yourself for your afternoon activities.
- If about now you're thinking, *I don't have time for this,* then you're definitely doing too much at work. Ask yourself if you want to be the pigeon or the statue.

ACTION ITEM

Mistake 6

Being Naive

*W*omen may not have the market on naïveté, but we certainly do our fair share of taking what people say at face value. The dynamic behind this is interesting. We often don't probe deeply to determine the veracity of what we're told, either because we don't want to embarrass the other person or because we want to see only the good in people. By busily focusing on the work itself, we often miss the more obvious behaviors that lie on the periphery.

Lisa was someone whose naïveté got her into trouble. She was the director of development for a nationally known nonprofit agency. Her department was efficient, there was a good sense of teamwork and camaraderie among the staff, and every year that Lisa was at the helm they surpassed their fund-raising goals—until she hired Adam, that is. He was the son of one of the board members, and her colleagues at the agency warned her it was not a good idea to hire him. Lisa was sure that if she established ground rules and kept the lines of communication open with Adam, it would work out just fine.

Within a few months the team began to falter. Morale was spiraling down. Team members weren't hitting their monthly targets. Several team members confided in Lisa that Adam was bad-mouthing her behind her back and spreading lies about her. Lisa's manager called her into his office several times to discuss the unrest on her team. For the first time in her career, she was seen as a less-than-capable leader.

When she openly discussed the problem with Adam, he denied doing anything to undermine her authority. She wanted to believe him and reiterated her expectations of him. The problem only went from bad to worse. Board members were beginning to question the head of the agency about problems they were hearing. Finally, Lisa left the agency for a better position, but not one she would have considered before Adam had come along.

When we see naïveté in another person, we often find it refreshing. Sometimes young people just beginning their careers benefit from it by making others want to mentor them or show them the rules of the road. When we see it in a more seasoned professional, however, we use it to discredit them. A woman's expression of naïveté underscores her inability to read a situation appropriately or learn from her experience.

COACHING TIPS

- If something doesn't make sense to you, ask for an explanation. If someone downplays your need for an explanation, be suspicious.
- Without assuming the worst, get in the habit of asking yourself what a person's motives might be.
- Don't rely on just one person's expertise when making major decisions. Solicit input from several reliable sources.
- If you find yourself the only person in the room who disagrees with the consensus *It can't be done,* and think, *But I could make it happen,* an alarm should go off that you're being naive.
- Trust your instincts. If it looks like a duck, sounds like a duck, and walks like a duck—it's a duck.

ACTION ITEM

Mistake 7

Pinching Company Pennies

$\mathcal{A}$ccustomed to having to account for how they spend their money, it seems even women who aren't hesitant to spend *their own* money on themselves fall into the trap of pinching company pennies. They allow themselves to be inconvenienced, or deny themselves the smallest item, for fear of spending a few extra dollars of the company's money on legitimate business expenses. Some women wear their savings as a badge of honor—when in most cases the amount of money they save is rounding off numbers for their corporation.

I was reminded of the folly of this when a woman executive told me about being delayed in Los Angeles for a flight to JFK. She was originally going to take a train to her hometown where her husband would pick her up but, with the delay, it would be too late to catch the last train. She struggled with how to get home in the most economical way possible—she even considered asking her husband to pick her up at 2 A.M. to save cab fare. Now, *that's* a mistake! A man wouldn't hesitate to call a car company or take a cab at that hour—regardless of the expense.

When you pinch pennies, you're wasting time and energy on meaningless matters. Additionally, you're more likely to be viewed as someone who isn't ready to play in the big leagues, and you definitely aren't taking care of one of the company's greatest assets—*you.*

COACHING TIPS

- When considering an expenditure, look at the big picture and how much difference the expense will really make in the larger scheme of things.
- If you have a budget—use it. Few companies reward, let alone notice, employees for being frugal.
- Consider the payoffs for spending small amounts of money on employees. A lunch here or a floral arrangement to a staff member in the hospital won't break the budget, but it will reap dividends in terms of goodwill and loyalty.
- Unless you're directed otherwise, never ask permission to spend money. Instead, expect you'll be told if there's a problem . . . and if there is, don't apologize. Simply acknowledge your understanding of the message and ask for clarification around spending authority.
- When the voice comes into your head that says, *I'm not sure I should spend this money*, talk back to it by asking, *What's the cost [in terms of time, resources, or money] of not spending it?*

ACTION ITEM

Mistake 8

Waiting to Be Given What You Want

$\mathcal{I}$ frequently hear women express disappointment over not having their needs met without having to ask. I don't get it. Ever hear the saying, *The squeaky wheel gets the grease?* On the other hand, if you're one of those people who, no matter *what* you're given, it isn't enough, you might find people resisting your constant requests. Still, more often women are made to *feel* like they're asking for too much when, in fact, they're not. If you won't ask, you don't risk hearing no, but you also won't get what you want.

The most obvious examples of this come when women finally get up the nerve to ask for a raise. They're frequently made to feel they're doing something wrong or have no right to ask for what is rightfully theirs. Having worked in human resources for many years, I know that men take care of their own needs but will often minimize what women are worth or owed. The average woman in the United States earns twenty-eight dollars less per hundred than her male counterparts. The figures are even more bleak for African American women and Latinas. African American women earn only sixty-five cents for each dollar their male counterparts earn; Latinas, fifty-two cents per dollar vis-à-vis Latino men. Although part of this discrepancy is clearly due to discrimination, another part is because disenfranchised groups are less likely to *ask* for what they want.

A client once called to tell me that she hadn't received the same signing bonus everyone else had already gotten as the result of transferring to a newly formed department. I inquired as to why she thought this happened. As people often do when confronted with a situation they don't understand, she made up a story in her head that it must have something to do with not being respected or just treating her as if she were invisible. It bothered her so much that she was losing sleep over it. Obviously, she needed to do something about it, but she was hesitant to "rock the boat."

After much discussion, we scripted out what she could say to her human resource manager to find out about the missing bonus. The way she *wanted* to put it was to ask whether she was entitled to a bonus. Typical girl behavior—never assume you're entitled to something you've been promised! My tip to her was not to ask, but to assume she was entitled to the bonus and find out why she hadn't received it. Essentially, she went in and said, "My signing bonus wasn't in my check for the past two pay periods and I'm wondering when I can expect to receive it."

Lo and behold, it had nothing at all to do with respect or being a woman. He had made a mistake. Of all the people who had transferred over, she was the only one who was due a performance review and annual raise within the next several weeks. He decided to wait on giving her the bonus so that he could do all the paperwork at one time. When her performance review was postponed because of the new assignment, though, he had forgotten to put in for the bonus. If she hadn't asked, she would have continued to be distracted by and lose sleep over this apparent slight.

The lesson for her was twofold. First, rather than make up a negative story, get the facts. Second, don't wait to be given what's owed to you—ask for it.

COACHING TIPS

- Mentally prepare requests in advance. Think about what you want and why you want it. When asking, be direct, straightforward, and accompany each request with two or three legitimate reasons why you should be given it. Try using the DESCript provided under Mistake 68.

- Consider the value of using the negotiation technique of fait accompli. That is, couch your request in the form of a statement. For example, rather than say, "I'd like to ask for an additional ten thousand dollars for next year's training budget," say, "I've added ten thousand dollars to the training budget. Additional staff and new technology account for the increase."

- Take a negotiation skills class or read *Essential Managers: Negotiating Skills* by Tim Hindle and Robert Heller. It's not only for managers and provides plenty of solid tips for how to negotiate effectively.

- Read *The Shadow Negotiation: How Women Can Master the Hidden Agendas That Determine Bargaining Success*, by Deborah Kolb and Judith Williams. The authors describe common negotiation problems encountered by women and give realistic suggestions for how to overcome them. The book also illuminates some of the hidden agendas that often accompany trying to get what you want.

- Separate being liked and getting what you deserve—they are mutually exclusive.

- Carefully choose your times for asking for what you want or deserve. Asking for a raise after layoffs is not a good idea. Nor is asking for a transfer to another department in the middle of a crucial project—it will make it look like you're trying to get out of work. Timing is everything in life—make sure you time your requests.

ACTION ITEM ☐

Mistake 9

Avoiding Office Politics

*R*epeat after me: "Politics is not a four-letter word." Trying to avoid office politics is like trying to avoid the weather. Like it or not, it is what it is. Politics is how things get done—in the workplace, in government, in professional organizations. If you're not involved in office politics, you're not playing the game, and if you're not playing the game, you can't possibly win.

The business of politics is simply the business of relationships and understanding the quid pro quo (something in exchange for something else) inherent to every relationship. Just as on Capitol Hill, careers are made or broken in the workplace based on relationships. And *when you need a relationship, it's too late to build it.* You've got to be building relationships all the time and with all kinds of people.

A successful workplace relationship, whether with a boss or a coworker, is one in which you clearly define what you have to offer and what you need or want from the other person. It happens all the time without putting a name to it. Consider your relationship with your best friend. You may need counsel from her or you may want company, a racquetball partner, or a variety of other things. If she gives you those, you're more likely to want to give her what she needs or wants. It may never be discussed, but the trade is implicit in the relationship. Workplace politics is no different. Each time you go out of your way for someone or give them what they need, you've earned a figurative "chip" that you can later cash in for something you need.

COACHING TIPS

- Approach political situations as you would any negotiation. Take time to find out what the other person needs, what you have to offer, and how you can facilitate a win–win situation.
- Remember: The quid pro quo of politics is *something in exchange for something else*. Don't just give in; think about what you want in exchange. Don't be afraid to cash in your chips.
- You can often win in the long run by giving up the smaller, less important points. When you do, you bank currency to be used at a later time.
- Don't avoid what you perceive to be a political problem. People will only go around you. Work through political situations in a way that allows others to see you as a problem *solver*, not a problem.
- Read *The Secret Handshake: Mastering the Politics of the Business Inner Circle*, by Kathleen Kelley Reardon. It's the best book I've read yet on the unspoken factors related to how things really get done in business and ways to understand the hidden rules that must be followed if you are to successfully maneuver through the political terrain of the workplace.

ACTION ITEM

Mistake 10

Being the Conscience

 $\mathcal{T}$ he terrorist attacks of September 11th and the recent spate of shady corporate financial dealings give us three extreme examples of women being the conscience—only to find they were ignored, stonewalled, or crucified. First, Enron's global finance vice president, Sherron Watkins, warned company president, Kenneth Lay, about her discomfort with the firm's accounting practices long before the company's demise. In August 2001 she had written a memo to Lay complaining about a "veil of secrecy" surrounding private investment partnerships at the firm. "I am incredibly nervous that we will implode in a wave of accounting scandals," wrote Watkins. "We are under too much scrutiny and there are probably one or two disgruntled 'redeployed' employees who know enough about the 'funny' accounting to get us in trouble." Unfortunately for Lay, and thousands of other Enron employees, he didn't heed her warning.

Cynthia Cooper of WorldCom's financial auditing department felt she had no choice but to go to the board of directors to report the misappropriation of massive amounts of money when her management told her to ignore inappropriate accounting procedures. This, of course, was the beginning of the end for the prestigious conglomerate. Although she received praise from strangers for her courage, coworkers blamed and shunned her.

Then there was FBI staff attorney Coleen Rowley who became the conscience of the agency after coming forward to speak the truth about inappropriate handling of evidence of terrorist activity prior to the attacks of September 11th. Even though the public lauded her and in 2002 *Time* magazine named her one of three

"Persons of the Year" (along with Watkins and Cooper), she was treated as a pariah by fellow FBI staffers.

Is this to say women shouldn't act in concert with their conscience and, at times, moral and ethical standards? Not at all. But women are far more likely than men to point out variance between company policy and practice. Most men have no difficulty with bending the rules as needed and when it's a case of "no harm, no foul." Let me give you an example. Claudette was an executive assistant for the vice president of consumer relations at a large entertainment company. Her boss routinely arrived late for work and expected that Claudette would cover for him. When the division president would call at nine-thirty, she would feel uncomfortable saying that her boss was "in a meeting" or had "stepped away from the desk." In her mind, the company start time was nine o'clock, and he should have been there on time. Similarly, if he was tardy in completing the required weekly expense report, he would change the dates to the current week so that he could be reimbursed for expenses incurred earlier in the week or month.

At first she would remind the boss of the rules, and he would cajole her into stretching them. After a short time working for this boss, Claudette went to human resources to complain. She felt the boss was asking her to compromise her values and ethics through these actions. Human resources, on the other hand, understood that the norms for this particular company were not very stringent and that she should be more cooperative with her boss if she wanted to build a successful relationship with him.

Unable to shift from her rigid interpretations, she finally asked for a transfer to another boss. Human resources was happy to oblige, but knew that Claudette would encounter the same problem with most of the executives at the company. What her boss asked her to do wasn't that unusual—nor was it unethical or immoral. Although she was eventually transferred to another boss who was known to be more of a straight arrow, human resources now branded her as somewhat of a prude and was aware of the limitations they would encounter in promoting or transferring her in the future.

The point of the story is, you need to weigh the benefit of pointing out minor infractions in company policy or procedure in light of the potential consequences. Sherron Watkins, Cynthia Cooper, and Coleen Rowley are to be admired for acting in concert with their consciences. In their cases the consequences were enormous for the company, the country, and them. Most of us, however, simply need to understand the realities of the workplace.

COACHING TIPS

- The workplace isn't a platform. Don't use it to further your cause.
- Don't equate doing *good* with doing *right* for yourself. Taking a controversial position on an issue may make you feel better—but except in unique situations it's not likely to get you ahead.
- Choose your battles carefully. Ask yourself if the risk of being the conscience is worth the potential profit. There will definitely be times when it is worth the risk—make it a calculated one.

ACTION ITEM

Mistake 11

Protecting Jerks

I don't know what it is about women and jerks. We're like jerk flypaper. Not only do we attract them more than men do, but we also tolerate them longer. In our usual attempt to avoid making others feel bad, we let them take up more of our time than we should, shoulder the blame for their mistakes, and make excuses for their behavior. Men seem to have a much better detection device when it comes to jerks. They smell them a mile away—and avoid them at all costs.

Greta is a good example of how women protect jerks. She works as a regulatory specialist on Wall Street. Her job is to ensure that trades are lawful and within the guidelines established by her nationally known firm. Greta reports to a jerk. He knows nothing about the regulations, but it doesn't stop him from continually telling her how to do her job—and often giving her and others wrong information that could create substantial liability for the company. Despite Greta's attempts to tell him he's wrong, he insists that she follow his directives.

When the department vice president asked why so many errors were made on several recent trades, she refused to say she was simply following the instructions of her boss. As a result, her performance review moved her down a notch on the rating scale, and her pay was reduced accordingly. Her efforts to protect her boss not only backfired on her, but also put the company in jeopardy of being fined for regulatory violations.

COACHING TIPS

- Trust your instincts. When you think someone is a jerk, he or she probably is.
- Distance yourself from jerks. Don't be found guilty by association.
- Politely but firmly tell a jerk to take a hike (more on this under Mistake 90).
- When you get blamed for the actions of some jerk, don't hesitate to redirect your accuser to the real source (which is what Greta should have done). Try saying something like, "I can see why you would be upset over this. Why don't you speak with Chris about it to find out why he wanted it done that way?"
- When the jerk is your boss, it's time to look for another job. Research conducted by the Center for Creative Leadership reveals that trying to change your boss is a waste of time. Employees don't change bosses' behaviors. So stop wishing he or she will change and put your own needs first.

ACTION ITEM

Mistake 12

Holding Your Tongue

*F*earful of hearing the accusation that we're too aggressive or pushy, women will often avoid saying things that should legitimately be said. How many times have you withheld comment, only to have a male colleague be applauded for saying exactly what you were thinking? Keep in mind that the accusations of being too pushy are *designed* to keep you quiet. They're ploys to make you feel bad about having an opinion or alternative viewpoint. Holding your tongue only serves to make you frustrated and appear less willing than you really are to speak up for what you believe.

Take Marilyn, for example. She was embroiled in an e-mail war with a colleague who had a reputation for being Teflon-like. Nothing stuck to him because he was so busy pointing the finger at others. For a while she spent most of her time placating him so she wouldn't be blamed, but he eventually got around to her. When I asked her why she didn't just tell him she felt the blaming wasn't doing any good and they should focus on the problem instead, she said she didn't want to fuel the fire any further. My suggestion to her was that the next time he started pointing the finger, she should turn it into a problem-solving discussion. She could say something neutral such as, "Blaming won't get us anywhere, Joe. Let's talk about how we can fix the problem of communication between our two departments." Even if his retort is, "I'm not blaming, I'm just looking for the cause of the problem," she can be a broken record and say, "Be that as it may, I'm ready to move into the problem-solving phase."

An interesting aside to this situation is the fact that Marilyn is a fifty-year-old Italian woman from a very traditional Brooklyn background and married to a man significantly older than she. As we explored what got in the way of her coming up with this solution herself, it became clear that her traditional socialization caused her to acquiesce to "macho" men. I pointed out to her the name of the game is, *When in Rome, do as the Romans do*. In other words, it may be appropriate to back off at home with her husband or with her father because that is the rule of her family, but at work the rules are different.

COACHING TIPS

• Disagree without being disagreeable. You can do this by first acknowledging what the other person said, then giving your opinion. It sounds like this: "If I understand you correctly, you think we should put Joe on the Stanford account. I propose we consider several other more qualified staff." Be prepared to back this up with two or three good reasons.

• Take more risks with giving your opinions at meetings. Practice giving your opinion at least once during every meeting. It gets easier every time you do it.

• Don't disregard the customs and traditions of your ancestors, but be more selective about how, when, and where you apply them.

• To counterbalance the feeling of being too aggressive, after you've expressed your opinion you could add an inquiry. For example, "That's how I see it. I'm curious to know what others think."

ACTION ITEM

Mistake 13

Failing to Capitalize on Relationships

A woman consultant was having difficulty selling her idea for a new book to a publisher. As we talked about how she might go about getting the attention of a particular editor, she mentioned that her father, an internationally known leader in his field, had a good relationship with this man. When I asked why in the world she didn't mention this to the editor, she said that she didn't want to capitalize on her father's name. This is yet another way women play differently than men. Men rely on relationships to open doors for them; they don't view it as taking advantage of anyone. For Pete's sake, it's why they build relationships in the first place!

There's a difference between name-dropping and using a relationship to help open a door. It's a reality that relationships sell everything from cars to consulting services. We do business with, and trust the judgments of, people we like. As opposed to guilt by association, it's success by affiliation. Don't be afraid to connect the dots among people in your network.

COACHING TIPS

- Ask permission to use a colleague's name when you're trying to get the attention of someone. For example, "I heard you mention Ellen Torres in past conversations. I'm trying to schedule a meeting with her and wonder if it would be all right to mention that I know you?"
- Ask for introductions. If there's someone you'd like to know at a meeting or party, ask the person organizing the event to make an introduction.
- Introduce people with like interests or needs. Doing so models the behavior you would like returned in kind.
- Ask for referrals. If you're looking for a job or just information, ask people if they know someone to whom they can refer you and if you can use their name when making the call.
- Read *Overcoming Your Strengths: 8 Reasons Why Successful People Derail and How to Remain on Track*, by yours truly, Lois P. Frankel. There's an entire chapter on relationship building and tips you won't find in this book.

ACTION ITEM

Mistake 14

Not Understanding the Needs of Your Constituents

*F*ormer British prime minister Margaret Thatcher was raised by a father who always told her to think for herself and not be swayed by the opinion of others. She learned this lesson so well that it earned her the nickname of Iron Lady. This strength became her ultimate downfall, however, when she found herself embroiled in controversy after she proposed a tax on everyone who voted. Despite every indication that her constituents strongly opposed the tax, Thatcher told advisers who urged her to reconsider her position, "You turn if you want to. The Lady's not for turning."

Although we're not all politicians, we all have constituents. They're the people we serve. Whether we serve them through our services or our products, we must know what they need and expect if we're to be perceived as adding value. The trap many women fall into is thinking they know what's best for their constituents and therefore not asking the right questions on the front end.

Take Marge, a technical consultant to engineering firms. Marge is as bright as they come—sharp as a whip. She knows her business inside and out. Other consultants go to *her* for consultation. Several years ago Marge found that her business wasn't as successful as she wanted it to be. She would sell an initial project to a company, only to find that she didn't get repeat business.

One day a client with whom Marge had developed somewhat of a friendship asked if he could give her some feedback. When he told her that his company appreciated her expertise but not her rigidity, she was shocked. She thought she was offering the best advice possible and always had the best interests of the client in the forefront of her mind. Instead, she found that her unwillingness to listen to clients' practical needs and applications was impeding her from being seen as value added to a company. She was viewed as intractable and difficult to work with.

It was difficult for her to hear, but Marge was also smart enough to know that the feedback was a gift. If this man's firm felt this way, others must, too, but without telling her. Instead, like most dissatisfied clients they'd just stopped using her services. This was why she hadn't been able to grow her business the way she wanted to.

With one simple change, Marge was able to turn the situation around. Following the initial diagnosis of client needs and presentation of her ideas and recommendations, she would stop and ask for input. If her ideas were met with skepticism, rather than seeing this as client ignorance as to the "right" way to do things (and selling her ideas harder), she would shift to listening and asking more questions. She discovered that initial resistance was often due to miscommunication; further discussion helped bridge that gap. In some cases she found that although the client wanted to implement her ideas in a manner different from the way she envisioned it, the changes actually worked and were ones she could later use with other clients.

Marge is a terrific example of someone who, aware of her own intelligence and capability, could be contemptuous of others who may not have been as talented. The lesson here is that there's often more than one way to skin a cat. You must take care not to be a victim of your own success.

COACHING TIPS

- Be more concerned with doing the right thing than doing things right. It's not a sign of weakness to change your mind when data collected dictates it's the right thing to do.
- Be acutely aware of the needs of your constituents. Be sure to read Mistake 9, which discusses identifying your network relationships and recognizing the quid pro quo.
- Differentiate polling from understanding the needs of your constituents. Polling is what you do when you can't make a decision independently. (See Mistake 15 for more.) Understanding the needs of others is information you may or may not use to make decisions that impact them.
- When met with resistance, avoid the urge to oversell. It usually results in polarizing factions or creating win–lose situations. Instead, let resistance be your cue to back off and shift to active listening.

ACTION ITEM

Chapter 3

How You Act

In the play *As You Like It*, William Shakespeare reminds us:

> *All the world's a stage and all the men and women are merely players.*
> *They have their exits and their entrances and one man in his time plays many parts.*

Success in the world of business depends on your ability to know your part and how to play it. It may sound as if I'm suggesting you be phony or false, but that's not it at all. Just as actors and actresses are judged by how well they play their roles, we are judged by whether we understand the nuances of what it means to *act* professionally.

It could be argued that the behaviors described in every chapter constitute *how you act*. This chapter is somewhat different in that it focuses on the subtle, stereotypical ways in which women behave that contribute to an overall impression of their being less competent than they really are. As I've said before, any one of the behaviors alone would not be a deal buster—but put several of them together and they can divulge a woman's underlying naïveté, need for approval, and lack of self-confidence.

Mistake 15

Polling Before Making a Decision

*J*ennifer is a lead auditor with a Wharton MBA and just over five years' experience working for a *Fortune* 500 oil company. Her performance is acknowledged as superb. When a promotional opportunity became available, her name was one of those considered on a short list of candidates. The word on the street about her, however, was that she was unwilling or unable to make a move without first getting input from everyone around her. As a result, she wasn't viewed as someone who could take quick and decisive action. Making her a manager was out of the question.

I call this polling. Participative decision making is a good thing. The inability to act without knowing what everyone thinks and if they approve isn't. It's a technique women use to avoid later confrontation. If they can get approval on the front end, no one can criticize them on the back end. The fine line you walk is between being seen as a lone ranger who acts independently, without regard for the opinions of others, and someone who can't make her own decisions or isn't confident enough to act without external input. The ideal is to act interdependently, recognizing the value of alternative input.

COACHING TIPS

- Take more risks by acting without first getting input from your supervisor. Begin with small, low-profile decisions.
- Ask yourself what you have to lose by acting in an independent manner. Try to explore the internal mechanism that keeps you tied into approval. Once you know, you can tape over the old message.
- Don't let the pendulum swing entirely in the other direction. There are times when it's appropriate to seek extensive input and/or approval. These tend to center on high-profile decisions where significant cost or potential loss is involved.

ACTION ITEM

Mistake 16

Needing to Be Liked

I can't deny the fact you like me! Right now, you like me!" There is no better example of how the need to be liked can impede success than this exclamation from Sally Field upon winning the 1984 Best Actress Oscar for her work in *Places in the Heart*. Up until that time Ms. Field's body of work included the likes of *Gidget, The Flying Nun,* and Burt Reynolds's sidekick in *Smokey and the Bandit.* This acceptance-speech gaffe marked a turning point for her. From that point on she assumed more serious roles, moved into film directing and production, and changed how she communicated with the public.

Likability is a critical factor in your success. People get promoted, demoted, hired, and fired based on how likable they are. There's a little girl in all of us who wants to be liked—and there's nothing wrong with that. It's when the needs of the little girl overshadow the rational, adult woman that we get into trouble.

The desire to be liked is so strongly ingrained in some people that it becomes nearly impossible for them to act in any alternative manner. It's critical to understand the difference between being liked and being respected. If you're only concerned with being liked, you will most likely miss the opportunity to be respected. Your need to be liked will preclude you from taking the kinds of risks taken by those who are respected. Conversely, if you're only concerned with being respected and not liked, you lose the support of people you may need in your camp. Paradoxically, it's the people who are liked *and* respected who are most successful in the workplace.

COACHING TIPS

- Use self-talk to counter the need to have *everyone* like you *all the time*. It's an impossibility.
- Ask yourself where the inordinate need to be liked comes from. Questions such as *What am I afraid of happening if I'm just myself?* or *What was I taught in childhood about the importance of being liked?* can help you pinpoint what purpose needing-to-be-liked serves in your life. If you can find the answer to these and similar questions, you're more likely to be able to overcome it.
- Balance your inclination to serve others' needs with serving your own. Before agreeing to something you may not want to, ask yourself how much it will matter if the other person is a little annoyed.
- When people get angry or annoyed with us, it's often for the purpose of getting us to do what they want. Don't fall for the ploy.

ACTION ITEM

Mistake 17

Not Needing to Be Liked

 $\mathcal{N}$ o, your eyes aren't playing tricks on you. For many women, this mistake is the inverse to the need to be liked. Fear of being perceived as a pushover causes some women to adopt the attitude, *I'm not here to win a popularity contest*. Well—I'm here to tell you, *Yes, you are*. Dr. Sharon Mass, director of social services at Cedars-Sinai Medical Center, didn't believe me when I told her this. Now she's allowed me to use her name and situation as an example of how this phenomenon can get in your way of achieving your career goals.

Sharon has a heart of gold. She genuinely cares about people. She also happens to be brilliant and the best at what she does. Her problem when we first met was that people didn't know any of this. They viewed her as a perfectionistic taskmaster, focused on getting the job done rather than on the needs of her staff. An underlying fear was that if anyone saw how warm and empathic she really was, they might take advantage of it. As a result, she compensated by going in the opposite direction. Like many women, Sharon had to learn how to allow her human, more stereotypically feminine side to emerge while at the same time capitalizing on the best of her more stereotypically masculine style of management.

COACHING TIPS

- Listen to the audiotape, *Warming the Stone Child*, by Clarissa Pinkola-Estes. Not needing to be liked or not caring about how others perceive you can be the result of early-childhood experiences that cause you to put up barriers to relationships. If this sounds like you, you'll enjoy this story that makes the point: It's never too late to get your needs met.

- Disabuse yourself of the notion, *Familiarity breeds contempt*. It doesn't unless *you* allow it to.

- Listen to the little things. Everyone wants an ear.

- Read, *Working with Emotional Intelligence*, by Daniel Goleman. Although Goleman's first book, *Emotional Intelligence*, is a more generic description of the nontechnical factors required for success, this book is more broadly applicable to the workplace. Goleman clearly describes the skill sets required for success, why they are important, and how you can develop them.

- Invest in building relationships. When you need a relationship, it's too late to build it.

ACTION ITEM

Mistake 18

Not Asking Questions for Fear of Sounding Stupid

*H*ow many times do we have to be told, *There are no stupid questions,* before we believe it? The problem is that we've come to rely on the old adage, *It's better to keep your mouth shut and look like a fool than to open it and confirm it.* Well, I disagree. There are so many ways in which women remain silent that we don't need to find any more. Asking a legitimate question (as opposed to making a statement couched as a question, which I'll talk about later) to ensure understanding is a sign more of confidence than of ignorance. If nearly three decades of working inside corporations has taught me anything, it's that if I don't understand something, most likely no one else does, either.

Women sometimes don't ask questions because they don't want to waste the group's time. Asking yourself the simple question, *Will the answer apply to only me?* should help you decide whether you should ask it. If the answer is yes, and you know you will have the chance to ask it following the meeting, then wait to ask your question off-line. If the answer is no, or you know you won't have the opportunity to ask again (the participants won't get together again or the speaker won't be available), then ask away. Do, however, be sensitive to the needs of the other participants in the meeting. If you've already asked several questions and you notice people getting fidgety or the meeting is running late, consider how critical it is that you get the answer just then.

COACHING TIPS

- If you don't get it, ask. It's far better than going off in the wrong direction.
- Observe people in meetings and you'll notice when others are confused or not understanding the message. Use this as an opportunity to help the group by saying something like, "I can tell by the looks on people's faces that it's not quite clear. Can you give us some examples or state it in other words?"
- Trust your instincts. If it doesn't seem clear, it's probably not.
- Use simple paraphrases as a way of gaining clarification. For example, "Do I understand you correctly that we're being given six months to complete phase one of the project, three months to complete phase two, and six months to complete phase three?" If you're wrong, you'll be told so; if not, you've gotten the information you need.
- If people make you feel stupid over a question you've asked, you can assume it's their problem, not yours. If they do it consistently, ask them point blank why they feel the need to put you down just because you've asked a question.

ACTION ITEM ☐

Mistake 19

Acting Like a Man

$\mathcal{T}$he emphasis in this mistake is on *acting*. Many women possess stereotypically male characteristics and behave accordingly. These women aren't acting; they're just being themselves. It can work for them. If you're not one of these people, don't start now. You'll never play the role of a man as well as you will a woman who plays her role well. At this point I hope you've gotten the idea that this book is about having a full arsenal of tactics and techniques at your disposal that are consistent with being a woman, not acting like a man.

Acting like a man in the workplace will inevitably get you into trouble. Just as we expect men to act in certain ways, we expect the same of women. When they don't, it creates a kind of dissonance. If behaviors don't match expectations, we tend to mistrust people or think they're not playing their role appropriately. Instead, you must play the role that's expected—while also widening the boundaries of the stage.

Being different from men isn't something to change or hide. We may be made to feel there's something wrong with how we act, but that's simply another ploy that's used to keep us in our places. Don't buy into it. Women bring a unique set of behaviors to the workplace that are needed, especially in today's climate. Our tendencies to collaborate rather than compete, listen more than talk, and use relationships rather than muscle to influence are the very same behaviors I coach men to acquire. But it's all about balance. Just as men can overuse their stereotypical characteristics, so can women.

A caveat of which to be aware is that behavioral norms for men and women vary among corporate cultures. One company I consult with has a strong norm that women and men must always act like ladies and gentlemen. I discovered this when I gave feedback to a woman that, if she wanted to be taken seriously, she needed to speak more loudly and be a bit more assertive when expressing her ideas. She responded—and other women in the meeting affirmed —that the company president didn't like aggressive women and she would be out of a job if she acted any differently. This particular woman had no problem conforming to the expectation because it was consistent with her character.

If by magic we plucked this woman up and set her down in another company—say, one where the norm is that *everyone* has to be aggressive to be heard—her behavior would not conform, and she would likely not experience the same success she currently enjoys. She would then have to decide whether she wanted to expand her behavioral skill set or find a culture more consistent with her natural tendencies where no changes would be needed. In most companies, however, the norm is a little less rigidly defined, and women have to find ways to expand the boundaries without being called out.

COACHING TIPS

- Continue to learn about your style, what works, where you get stuck, and ways you can complement your natural strengths with new behaviors. You can do this by asking for feedback, videotaping yourself in a meeting or giving a presentation, or taking a workshop on personal development. The Appendix includes several resources for workshops that I recommend.

- If you tend to be more aggressive and it's not working for you, read Jean Hollands's book *Same Game, Different Rules: How to Get Ahead without Being a Bully Broad, Ice Queen, or "Ms. Understood."* The book points out that women often can't get away with the same behavior as men—and pretending that you can could ruin your career. You may have to decide whether it's more important to you to further your career or take on the system. I often hear women lament over this double standard, but it does exist and it is real.

- Modify the rules to meet your needs and others' expectations. Pounding the table and speaking loudly may not be acceptable, but being a broken record (saying the same thing over and over in different ways) can accomplish the same end.

- Be conscious of the fact that behavioral expectations vary among corporate cultures. What works in one company may not work in another. Be sure to observe the cultural norms and modify your style accordingly. If you can't bring yourself to act in a way that is acceptable, your best bet is to find a work environment that complements your natural style.

ACTION ITEM

Mistake 20

Telling the Whole Truth and Nothing but the Truth (So Help You God)

*W*hy is it that women, more so than men, feel the need to blurt out the truth about themselves, even if it's self-disparaging or damaging to them? A study was once done in which men and women were asked to describe themselves. The men, regardless of appearance, described themselves in factual and positive (or at least neutral) terms. "I'm six feet tall, brown hair, 195 pounds, and have a mustache," said one portly, aging man. Right. And I'm Julia Roberts. Women were more likely to use more pejorative phrases such as, "My hair is graying, I could stand to lose a few pounds, I'm not *too* bad looking . . ."

The same holds true when a woman is asked to debrief a particular project where something has gone askew. She'll blame herself and identify all the things she could have done differently. What do men do? Again, they're objective and Teflon-like in their descriptions. One man, when accused of designing an ill-conceived methodology, said, "The problem wasn't the methodology, it was that the methodology didn't reflect realistic measures of the process." And *who* designed the methodology to begin with?

Anne Mulcahy, chairman and CEO of Xerox, found out the hard way that telling the unadulterated truth can get you into trouble. At an investors conference early in her tenure she told the world that the company had "an unsustainable business model." The next day, Xerox stock lost 26 percent of its value. Mulcahy originally thought that since it was no secret the company was losing money, it naturally followed that there was a problem with the business model. "Looking back," said Mulcahy later, "I should have said, 'The company recognizes changes have to take place in the business model.'" She advises people to continue being straightforward, but also to make sure "you don't provide sound bites that can be used out of context . . ."

It seems Mulcahy hadn't yet learned the art of putting a "positive spin" on a situation. Telling the truth doesn't require you to cast yourself in a negative light. It requires an honest, objective description of facts without blame or self-flagellation.

COACHING TIPS

• Listen carefully to the question you're asked and answer it simply and objectively. The question, "Why wasn't the project done on time?" isn't an indication that the person expects you to point the finger at yourself. More than likely, there are good reasons why the project wasn't completed on time, and *this* is what you should offer in response. An appropriately honest response would be, "There are two primary reasons. First, we didn't have the staff required to meet the unrealistic deadline, and second, the information required to complete the data wasn't made available to us until two days before the deadline."

• Even when you legitimately bear responsibility for a blunder, don't make it worse by embellishing it. Avoid the tendency to agree or explain and, whatever you do, don't allow yourself to feel bad about it. We *all* make mistakes. Replace apologetic, explanatory, or defensive responses with more neutral ones. Practice saying, "I understand what you're saying and I'll keep that in mind in the future." You are neither agreeing nor disagreeing—simply acknowledging.

• Counter or pair every negative with a positive. This is what positive spin is all about.

Change This:

"I have to admit, I could have done a better job of making sure we remained under budget."

"I wish I had done a little more inquiry before making the final decision about that candidate."

"I don't think I'd be the right person for the job—I don't possess all the qualifications listed in the job description."

To This:

"Although we didn't come in under budget, we did complete the project ahead of schedule."

"Although the employee proved to be a bad match for the job, we learned a good lesson in what we really want."

"It's true I don't have *all* the qualifications listed, but what makes me a viable candidate is my depth of hands-on experience."

ACTION ITEM

Mistake 21

Sharing Too Much Personal Information

$\mathcal{T}$his mistake is actually an extension of telling the truth to an inappropriate degree. The woman who shared this thought with me was a manager who noticed that the women in her department were much more likely than men to reveal complicated personal situations that could later be used against them. The example she gave was of a woman in her department who was experiencing performance problems on the job. At a one-on-one meeting the employee broke down crying and told a long, involved story about how her mother was dying, her sisters wouldn't assume any responsibility, the burden fell on her to make all the health-care decisions, her husband was out of a job . . .

Relevant? Yes, but more than her boss needed to know. It gave the boss the impression she couldn't handle stress well. When a project came up that the boss knew would be stressful, she didn't want to take the risk of giving it to this employee. Sharing personal information isn't in and of itself a mistake—it's sharing *too much* of it that can come back to bite you.

COACHING TIPS

- Be selective about the personal information you share and with whom you choose to share it.
- If you're a manager or supervisor, be even more careful. The rule of thumb I recommend is, *Be the best friend you can be to your employees, but don't think for a minute they're your best friends.*
- Whether you're a manager or not, don't entirely withhold personal information. I've seen women do this, and it backfires. It makes you look secretive or dishonest. Sharing appropriate amounts of personal information enables others to see the human side of you and, in turn, builds relationships.
- When a personal situation is impacting your ability to perform your job, be honest, but be brief. It's enough to say, "I'm going through a rough time right now but my job is important to me. I'll work on paying closer attention to the details."

ACTION ITEM

Mistake 22

Being Overly Concerned with Offending Others

$\mathcal{A}$n interesting phenomenon I've observed is when a man is controversial or offers a different viewpoint, neither men nor women respond as if they've been offended. They may be angry or hurt, but the man is rarely accused of acting inappropriately. Because women are more likely to encounter resistance by being told they're out of line, they tend to agree (even when they don't really agree) and fail to confront tough issues.

This is just another one of those ploys people use against us—and we unwittingly buy into it. If someone acts offended by a legitimate request or concern of yours, the implied message is that you've acted inappropriately or done something wrong. As a result, they know you're more likely to back down. When you back down often enough, you've trained others to feign offense as a defensive posture. It becomes a self-defeating catch-22.

Karl Marx used the term *mystification* to refer to the process whereby those with power and affluence denied the fact that there was a problem between the social classes, then denied they were denying. Here's how it sounds at work:

EMPLOYEE: It's been two years since I've had a raise and I'd like to talk to you about why I think I deserve one.

HR MANAGER: Are you accusing me of overlooking your well-being?

EMPLOYEE: No, I'm not accusing you of anything, I just want to talk about getting a raise.

HR MANAGER: Well, you obviously think there's a problem.

EMPLOYEE: In fact, I do think there's a problem with not getting a raise in two years, but I'm not blaming you.

HR MANAGER: We have a system in place that ensures our staff is fairly treated.

EMPLOYEE: But if I haven't gotten a raise, then the system isn't working. I don't think you see that from your perspective.

HR MANAGER: Now you're saying I don't see the problem.

Get the picture? This is a convoluted and circuitous method that never quite solves the problem and causes women to back down or not even try to bring up sensitive topics for fear of offending someone.

COACHING TIPS

- Use the DESCript (see Mistake 68) to prepare for difficult conversations.
- Read *Difficult Conversations: How to Discuss What Matters Most,* by Douglas Stone et al. If you're one of those people who avoid confrontations because you're afraid of hurting someone's feelings, you'll find terrific guidance for how to say what must be said and in a way that won't damage the relationship.
- When expressing a controversial or different viewpoint, use the technique of contrasting what you do want and what you don't want: "I don't want to make it appear I haven't heard what you said, because I have. I do want to express a different way to look at the situation."
- Let the other person know when what you're about to say is difficult for you by beginning your sentence with, "This is a bit difficult for me to say, but I do want to let you know how I see the situation." This cues most people to be more patient with you.
- If you know you've expressed yourself inoffensively, and the other person is still offended, don't acquiesce. Instead, respond with a simple acknowledgment of his or her feelings—"I can see you feel offended by this"—and revert to listening. Avoid the inclination to backpedal and negate your true sentiments.

ACTION ITEM

Mistake 23

Denying the Importance of Money

$\mathcal{I}$ know all the statistics about gender disparity in pay and benefits. You probably do, too. I don't want to downplay the significance of these factors—they're real and they're relevant. But unless you're an equal-pay activist, you have no control over those factors. The real question then becomes, *What are you going to do about it?*

Money is power, and power is something women misinterpret and avoid. Ask a woman if she's powerful and she'll give you five reasons why she's not. This translates into feeling uncomfortable with the subject of money and thinking she actually deserves less than she's due. Or worse yet, she doesn't give money a second thought except in terms of needing enough to pay the bills.

A friend of mine and I often joke, "What are we doing wrong?" when we hear about people who earn exorbitant sums of money or make extravagant purchases. Given that we've both chosen helping fields (she's a psychotherapist), we know we've spent our careers focusing on things other than money. Although I'm quite content knowing I make a difference, this shouldn't be mutually exclusive of making a living.

It's a fact that you get what you focus on. If you're not earning a fair salary or not being given the raises you deserve, it's time to focus on money. It won't mean you're any less committed to your work—only that you're equally committed to your well-being and that of your family.

COACHING TIPS

• If you think you're underpaid, do research into the pay ranges typical for your job or industry. You can do this on-line, through a professional association, or by asking trusted friends at other companies what their ranges are (don't ask what they earn). Because salaries differ from city to city and field to field, I can't give you a Web site that is comprehensive, but from your browser type in "salary surveys" and you'll be given a host of choices.

• If it turns out that you *are* underpaid, use logic and facts to make a case for why you should get a raise. Ask a friend to help you practice delivering the message.

• Subscribe to (and make a point of reading) a magazine that focuses on money and career issues. Several to consider are *Fortune*, *Money*, and *Smart Money*.

• Overcome the notion that talking about money is crass or impolite.

• Join, or start, a women's investment club.

ACTION ITEM

Mistake 24

Flirting

*H*ow many thousands of women have met the person of their dreams at work, fallen in love, and gotten married? It happens all the time and it's not such a bad thing, but it is a potentially dangerous one. Just ask Monica Lewinsky. Or Mary Cunningham. (Remember the William Agee–Mary Cunningham scandal at Bendix Corporation?) A headline in the September 27, 1998, *Seattle Times* read, OFFICE SEX ALMOST NEVER PUTS CEOS OUT OF WORK. But what happens when you're not a CEO?

I once coached a woman whom everyone assumed was having an affair with the department manager. Whether she was could never be determined, but that wasn't the point. Her behavior toward him led others to believe she was having an affair with him—and perception is reality. Her flirting, which caused others to be suspicious of their relationship, took the form of laughing a little too loud at his bad jokes, offering to run errands for him, siding with him in meetings when others expressed a different viewpoint, and inviting him to lunch at least once a week (when most others—both men and women—worked through their lunch hours).

What's a little harmless flirting, you ask? We know people find partners at work all the time. The harm is that it's the women who flirt—not the men—who most often become the butt of office jokes and who are more likely to suffer the consequences. In the case above, people excluded her from the grapevine (an important source of information) and other discussions to which she should have been privy for fear she would share the information with the boss. It reduced their trust in her and diminished her ability to perform effectively.

Another woman learned from her 360-degree feedback report

that her peers thought she flirted too much. The feedback floored her because she had no inkling how others could perceive that. Then one day I happened to see her at lunch with her boss and understood perfectly. As he chatted away confidently, she smiled and listened with her head slightly tilted. I could see how it might be perceived as flirting, but what it really came down to was that the woman came from a traditional Irish family where she'd learned to acquiesce to men. Her way of showing respect to men, whether in one-on-one situations or in meetings, was to "dumb down" in her actions and words.

COACHING TIPS

• Don't overtly flirt with coworkers. Knowing glances, whispered conversations, and laughing at stupid jokes don't belong in the workplace.

• If you *are* dating or having an intimate relationship with a coworker, be discreet. Conduct your personal business outside work and work-related activities.

• Don't be so naive as to think you can keep these things secret for long. There's nothing wrong with dating a coworker—just be up front about it.

• When you become personally involved with the boss (or—if you are the boss—with an employee who directly reports to you), you're playing with fire. Seriously consider the personal and professional risks and don't hesitate to get outside counseling if needed.

ACTION ITEM ☐

Mistake 25

Acquiescing to Bullies

*I*t's not often I run into bullies. Most people in corporations know how to express themselves tactfully and diplomatically, seeking to solve problems, not create new ones. Such was not the case in a recent meeting with a vice president, however, who was clearly angry that he had been inadvertently double-billed for a particular service. None of the usual techniques for defusing difficult situations worked. I listened, paraphrased, reflected his feelings . . . and none of it made a difference. Finally, I said, "I'm not accustomed to being personally attacked." A third person in the meeting tried to intervene by saying, "I think you're getting defensive, Lois." To which I calmly replied, "When I'm personally attacked, I get defensive." After the meeting, the person who intervened said he thought I could have handled it differently. My response was, "The guy is a bully and I wanted him to know I wouldn't be intimidated."

When we're bullied, we do one of two things: counterattack or acquiesce. Neither serves to shift the dynamic. By simply letting someone know how you feel, you stand a better chance of eliminating the offensive behavior—something that will never happen if you acquiesce. Even if the behavior doesn't change, you've put the person on notice that you won't tolerate it and, as such, you've maintained your self-respect. By the way, the dynamic did change after my remark to this bully, and we were ultimately able to find a solution that met his needs.

COACHING TIPS

- Use the techniques I mentioned—(listening, paraphrasing, reflecting feelings)—as a place to begin defusing a bully. More often than not, they work.
- Don't roll over and play dead when someone tries to intimidate you. It's a tactic some people regularly use to make their point or get their way. Ask yourself what you're feeling in that moment and express it as an *I* message. Rather than "You're not listening to me," say, "I feel I'm not being heard." It's less accusatory, and no one can argue with your feelings.
- Turn the discussion to problem solving by acknowledging what you've heard and asking what the person would like to do: "I understand that you're frustrated with the fact that the shipment has not yet gone out. Let's talk about what we can do to get it to you as soon as possible."
- Avoid the inclination to apologize. If apologies are appropriate, you can always do so later. Apologizing to a bully only fuels the fire and reinforces the notion that you are a victim.

ACTION ITEM

Mistake 26

Decorating Your Office Like Your Living Room

*O*ffices are often an extension of your home. In many cases, women spend more time there than they do in their own living rooms. Nevertheless, this doesn't mean that your office should look like your living room. More so than men, women love the aesthetics involved with decor and frequently want to create a warm and comfortable setting, not only for themselves but for those who enter their work space as well.

I've been in the offices of women who've replaced overhead lighting with table and floor lamps (creating a more ambient environment) and scattered overstuffed couches, throw pillows, and personal memorabilia throughout their space. Depending on the message you want to convey, this can work for or against you. I don't recommend it for most women. It's more appropriate for people responsible for counseling employees than it is for those in other positions.

At the other extreme is someone like Christine, a physician at a metropolitan hospital, who had *nothing* on her walls. At our first coaching session I was struck by how austere and cold her work space was. As we worked together and I received feedback from her staff, I realized that this was simply a reflection of her personality. One of my coaching tips to her was to warm up her office with family pictures and artwork that would humanize her space.

Yes, your office or work space can be a reflection of who you are and what's important to you. But unless you're an interior decorator by profession, it doesn't pay. By emphasizing your femininity, you diminish your credibility.

COACHING TIPS

- The decor of your office should be consistent with the kind of firm in which you work. In a more conservative culture you should select artwork, colors, and furniture that are tasteful and understated. More creative fields can tolerate a bolder approach.
- Given that your office or work space makes a statement about you, do pay attention to decor. In most offices you're assigned furniture, but how you accessorize it is up to you. Choose accessories that reflect your personality without overly emphasizing the feminine side of you.
- If you lean toward minimalism, then minimally have family pictures or other photographs displayed where people can see them. They serve to humanize you and act as conversation starters. One single woman I know has a framed picture of her dog on her desk.
- Look at your office with fresh eyes. If someone very special were coming to visit you at work, what would you change? Why? What adjectives would you attach to your work space if you didn't know who worked there? Are those the adjectives you want to be used about you?
- Keep your visible work space neat and clean. It conveys the impression of being organized and on top of things.

ACTION ITEM

Mistake 27

Feeding Others

$\mathcal{U}$nless you're Betty Crocker, there shouldn't be home-baked cookies, M&Ms, jelly beans, or other food on your desk. Hillary Rodham Clinton may have been lambasted for her comment about not staying home and baking cookies, but her point was well taken. We don't ascribe a sense of impact or import to people who feed others. It may seem like a small or inconsequential thing, but the fact is, you rarely see food on men's desks.

The act of feeding is equated with nourishing, and nourishing is *definitely* a stereotypically female attribute. Additionally, food on the desk is often an invitation to stop and chat a moment (people can't just "eat and run"). Combined, the aspects of feeding and encouraging conversation emphasize stereotypically feminine qualities.

There are, of course, exceptions to every rule, and this is one of them. Lise Dewey, manager of training and development at Universal Entertainment, told me she often coaches her own employees (especially men) who are perceived by others to be a bit *too* brusque, domineering, or downright abrasive (emphasis on the word *too*) to put a candy dish on their desks. The reason is obvious—she wants them to "warm up" their image and balance their more aggressive behaviors.

Similarly, Lise has a huge candy bowl on her own desk—in part because *she* wants to eat it (although you could never tell by looking at her) and in part because she is in a role where people often come to her office to discuss personal and confidential matters. The candy is designed to make people feel comfortable with her.

If you don't want to be perceived as stereotypical, think twice before putting food on your desk. This is especially true if you're a woman who makes many of the other mistakes contained in this book. As with many of the tips in this book, it isn't the food alone that's lethal—it's the combination of mistakes that diminishes your credibility.

COACHING TIPS

• Unless feeding people is a conscious strategy, just say no to feeding people at work.

ACTION ITEM

Mistake 28

Offering a Limp Handshake

*W*omen may not have the exclusive rights on this one, but we are more likely to hold back when offering our hand in greeting. For fear of appearing too masculine, we let the pendulum swing the other way. A handshake is how you make your first impression upon initially meeting someone. It says something about you before you ever open your mouth. Although you don't want to develop a bone-crushing grasp, you do want to be certain your handshake conveys the message, *I'm someone to be taken seriously.* One good pump and a concise greeting (such as "I'm delighted to finally meet you"), combined with solid eye contact, will do the trick.

COACHING TIPS

- Practice your handshake with both male and female friends or colleagues. Get their feedback about whether yours is too limp or too strong. You may have a different handshake for men than for women. Continue practicing until you find a place where both men and women tell you your handshake conveys the message you want it to.

- Here's a tip a colleague's father taught him when he was a young boy: Keep extending your hand until you hook thumbs (try it and you'll see how it works). Don't stop with just grabbing the fingers. (And by the way—how many fathers taught their daughters how to shake hands?)

- When meeting someone for the first time, if he or she doesn't offer a hand first, offer yours. It's a sign of confidence.

- Depending on the situation, you may want to convey a sense of sincerity or warmth. This may be the case when meeting someone in person for the first time after speaking by phone for some extended period. To do this, loosen the grip just a bit and briefly place your left hand on top of the person's right hand as it shakes yours. Again, practice this until it comes naturally.

- While I'm on the subject of greetings, the question often comes up as to whether it's appropriate to greet an associate with a hug. This one is tricky. My advice is to never hug someone unless he or she does so first. Not only is it a matter of invading another person's space, but it also softens the greeting.

ACTION ITEM

Mistake 29

Being Financially Insecure

*V*irginia Woolf said every woman must have a room of her own. There are other women who will tell you a bank account of your own is even more important. Whether you're dependent on a husband, a domestic partner, or an employer, financial dependence translates into a loss of career choices and power. Having no money of your own, having your financial affairs in disarray, or not adequately preparing for your financial future equates to having no freedom.

But why is this a potentially career-busting mistake? Because if you don't have financial security, you wind up acting in ways and making decisions counter to your best career interests. Women are more likely to remain in dead-end jobs and be forced to work beyond the normal point of retirement because they can't afford to leave. Women are less likely to make tough, but necessary, decisions because they're afraid to rock the boat and lose their jobs. And women are often less able to understand the financial implications of business decisions because they don't pay close enough attention to their own financial affairs—the place where they *should* be learning about financial matters and extrapolating the lessons to business.

Women are also often forced to reenter the workforce ill prepared for success because they were dependent on someone who decided to discontinue financial support. I fully understand that being a homemaker teaches a woman many skills that are directly applicable to a job, but try telling this to the hiring source. As a result, late entries to the workforce are at a career disadvantage and wind up in low-paying entry-level positions.

Carrie is just such a woman. She worked her entire life for one employer, and worked hard. She was single with no children and, although she owned her own home and created somewhat of a nest egg, by the age of sixty-two she still hadn't accumulated enough to retire. When the company was sold, the old managers who knew her and respected her work were all given golden parachutes to leave. Because she wasn't high enough up in the company, she was not one of the people offered this benefit.

As new managers took their place, she discovered the skills she had honed over the years weren't the same as those the new owners wanted in staff earning as much as she did. It wasn't so much that they could hire a younger person more cheaply; it was more a matter of hiring someone who more closely met their expectations. At her age and salary Carrie didn't have many choices. She was forced to remain in a company where she was no longer respected and do menial tasks for which she was overqualified because she hadn't planned properly for her financial future.

COACHING TIPS

- Read 9 *Steps to Financial Freedom: Practical and Spiritual Steps so You Can Stop Worrying*, by Suze Orman. In an interesting combination of practical financial advice and an insightful approach to understanding your financial attitudes, Orman provides a road map to overcoming your fears and misconceptions about money and investment.

- Select a good financial planner, and with his or her help develop a solid personal financial plan.

- If you don't already have one, go out today and open a savings account. It doesn't matter if you start it with fifty dollars or five hundred, do it. Then get into the habit of depositing as much money as you can afford on a weekly or biweekly basis.

- When you go to the store to purchase only a few items, pay with a twenty-dollar bill and put the change into a jar at home. When the jar is full, transfer the coins and dollar bills to your savings account.

- Open an IRA or other retirement account for yourself. Deposit into it the maximum allowed yearly. If you're over forty, create a budget that allows you to contribute even more.

ACTION ITEM

Mistake 30

Helping

*K*risten is a new manager. She prides herself on not asking anyone on her team to do anything she herself wouldn't. At a recent off-site where her team was working in small groups and she was shuttling among them to offer assistance, one group asked her to bring them coffee. Thinking this wasn't a big thing, she brought it. Then they asked her to make some copies of their work product, which she did. The final request was for fresh Magic Markers.

At first blush it doesn't seem like anything was wrong, but closer scrutiny reveals the reason why certain members of Kristen's team often miss deadlines and ignore her requests for information. In her desire to help her team, they had begun to view her as a functionary. While she was getting coffee, fetching Magic Markers, and making copies, several of the men on the team were providing the real leadership the group needed.

A study conducted in the early 1980s interviewed 135 women to determine, among other things, how women gain knowledge. The researchers found that many of the people with whom they spoke said helping others, through either providing assistance, listening, or teaching, actually gave them more insight into themselves and greater self-confidence. Why? Because women are taught early in their lives that others know more than they do, so knowledge and self-confidence must be attained *externally*. Helping others is one way capable women gain external validation for their self-worth. This certainly accounts for why so many women go into helping fields.

Although I'm a staunch believer in the servant leadership philosophy espoused by Robert Greenleaf, many women take this to the extreme and encounter the same problems as Kristen when they're promoted to the management ranks or asked to lead a project team. They fail to transition from doer to leader. If you're busy doing, you don't have time to provide the vision, guidance, technical support, and oversight required of a leader.

COACHING TIPS

- Read the *Harvard Business Review* article "What Leaders Really Do" by John Kotter. The article helps you to take a look at higher-order behaviors expected at the more senior levels of any organization. Even if you aren't there yet, reading this will help you to get there.
- Differentiate *helping* and *being used*. If you're truly helping, you're providing the resources and support needed to allow others to get the job done efficiently and effectively. If you're working harder than everyone else on your team or task force, you're being used.
- Rather than offering to do the work of another, offer to teach him or her how to do it. Even though it may take longer in the short term, it will pay dividends in the long term.
- Ask yourself if you're helping because you think you'll be liked for it, or because it's something you really want to do.
- If you're up for a dense and highly theoretical—but revealing—book about women's cognitive and emotional development, read *Women's Ways of Knowing: The Development of Self, Voice and Mind*, by Mary Field Belenky et al.

ACTION ITEM

Chapter 4

How You Think

Changing how you *think* about how you work is essential to changing self-defeating behavior. Most of us have notions about what will get us recognized and what won't. These are called *superstitious behaviors* because we come to believe that if we don't do them, something catastrophic will happen. *I'll only be rewarded if I work harder than everyone else* and *My boss will fire me if I tell her what I really think* are examples of superstitious thinking. These thoughts are often built around parental messages about work that may have been true for our parents but are no longer valid for us. Similarly, these behaviors may have been functional early in our careers, but they're usually not as helpful later. What we do as entry-level workers to get respect and attention is more related to the task at hand than it is to exhibiting behaviors related to leadership capability, relationship skills, and the like. It's thus difficult to relinquish these beliefs because they've worked—up until now.

One of the most difficult aspects of coaching is getting people to try new behaviors. It's a little like letting go of old worn-out tennis shoes. They're comfortable. You've broken them in. You know exactly how they're going to feel when you wear them. They looked great three years ago, but you can't wear them in public anymore. This next section focuses on some of those beliefs you may have formed early in your work life that need to be retired before you do.

Mistake 31

Making Miracles

*T*hink logically about this. When you look around at the people who get promoted and recognized, are they the people who make miracles? Women take pride in the fact they can do more with less, meet or beat impossible deadlines, and get juice out of a turnip. They actually believe others will recognize and appreciate their efforts. What they don't realize is that every time they make a miracle, they've set the bar higher in terms of what people expect from them. Not only that, but while they're busy jumping through hoops their male colleagues are doing things that give them more visibility and, ultimately, more rewards.

Take Anita, for example. She transferred from the advertising business into a Big Five consulting firm. Without a doubt she was an expert in her field—everyone said so. And as her boss said: "She inherited a mess." By coming in early, staying late, and working weekends she started to get a handle on the problem and made inroads into correcting it. No matter what was asked of her, Anita delivered.

Whereas the first year she could do no wrong, the next year she could do no right. People came to expect her to achieve the same results—and more—every day. To do this, Anita had to continue spending ridiculous amounts of time at the office. She had set the standard so high the first year that she couldn't possibly surpass it, as everyone expected, the second year—or even keep up the pace. This is not to say she shouldn't have given it her all the first year, or that she should in any way sacrifice excellence. It simply means that you must be realistic about establishing work habits and not thinking you have to be superwoman to be effective.

COACHING TIPS

- Manage people's expectations. Always be willing to go the extra mile, but don't be afraid to point out when something is unrealistic. Everyone always wants everything yesterday. Pushing back when you're being taken advantage of won't be a career buster.
- Set realistic daily or weekly goals. Women think there are thirty-four hours in every day. Remember Parkinson's Law: *Work expands to fill the time available*. If you come to work in the morning thinking you're going to work until 9 P.M., then you will. If you come in with the idea you're going to leave at 6 P.M., you'll probably be out not long after.
- If you're understaffed, *ask* for help or negotiate reasonable deadlines. You can always say, "I'd love to get this to you by five o'clock as requested but we don't have the staff to achieve that kind of turnaround. Tomorrow at five is more realistic." From there you may have to negotiate, but you're less likely to work until midnight.

ACTION ITEM

Mistake 32

Taking Full Responsibility

*T*his is a variation on the miracle theme. Just because you're assigned a project doesn't mean you're the only one who *can* do it or *should* do it. It only means you're the one responsible for making it *happen*. You get no brownie points for doing a project alone. You get brownie points for getting it done. In fact, you may be looked upon more favorably if you're able to delegate parts of the project or influence others to help you. It shows that you know how to manage a project. Haven't you ever noticed that when a man is given a project, the first thing he does is begin delegating?

Just recently I coached a woman who'd been given responsibility for developing a plan for corporate philanthropy. The company had never before funded grants to the nonprofit community. The thought of doing this was daunting to her. She had no idea where to start. As we discussed it, she began to realize she didn't have to do it all today—nor did she have to do it all herself. Engaging various stakeholders in the company and in the community would actually be better because she would get their buy-in from the start and could take advantage of their ideas, energy, and resources. She left the meeting feeling as if a burden had been lifted off her shoulders.

COACHING TIPS

- When assigned a project or task, avoid the tendency to start *doing*. Take time to think it through, plan it, identify resources, and so forth.
- Continually build relationships throughout your company and your professional community. When you need a relationship, it's too late to build it. I'll speak more to this a little later in this section.
- Don't reinvent the wheel. What I've come to realize is that there's not too much new under the sun. If *I* have to do something, it means other people must have done it before. Find these people and ask them to share their expertise.
- Learn to delegate. Even if you don't have staff reporting directly to you, call on the relationships you've built to help with providing assistance.

ACTION ITEM

Mistake 33

Obediently Following Instructions

*T*his isn't true of all women, but some of us, when given an assignment, become like dogs with a bone. We're so anxious to get the job done quickly that we can't see what's on the periphery that would help us work smarter. We tend to look at the details, not the big picture. People who get ahead know how to balance the tactical with the strategic.

There are two women in my office who are really good at this. Kim has her Ph.D. in cognitive psychology, and Majella is studying to be an illustrator. They were hired to manage the many new projects and clients that come through the door. Because I tend to see the big picture but not the details, I had in the past always assumed I needed to surround myself with detail-oriented staff and hired accordingly. Kim and Majella have shown me the error of my ways and have spoiled me for all time.

When given an assignment, rather than jumping in to immediately start it, both women begin by first thinking about it, then asking lots of good questions. This saves an incredible amount of time—not to mention money and frustration on their part—because we no longer get halfway down the road only to realize my original idea for the project was less than well thought through. They add value to the company by not obediently following my instructions but rather by thinking and planning—which is what *you* want to be known for.

COACHING TIPS

- Spend time brainstorming with creative colleagues before beginning complex or large assignments.
- Rather than responding to the details of an assignment, before beginning consider how it could be done faster, cheaper, or more effectively.
- Take a stress management class to overcome the need to treat every assignment with the utmost urgency.
- Learn to play chess. It will help you think more strategically.

ACTION ITEM

Mistake 34

Viewing Men in Authority as Father Figures

*C*arolyn was an upwardly mobile career woman who was smart and assertive—that is, with everyone except those men who were senior to her. When they asked her a question, she became tongue-tied and childlike. She came to coaching because she knew she wasn't projecting the image she wanted to with these men. She acted like a little girl and, in turn, she was treated like one. Early on I realized that giving her tips for being more assertive or speaking articulately wouldn't work. She already knew how to do that. The problem was, she couldn't do it with certain people.

During one of our early meetings I asked her to tell me about her father. As it turns out, he was a former colonel in the army and ran his family as he might a platoon. She described him as authoritative, critical, and impossible to please. When I inquired into how she survived childhood, she said she'd learned to be a good girl, obey all the rules, study hard, and not do anything that might displease him. When she entered the workforce, she responded to men senior to her as if they were her father and she, the dutiful daughter.

Conversely, Suzanne's father was nurturing, loving, and compassionate. He encouraged her to pursue her dreams and emotionally supported her in the process. She came to coaching because she couldn't understand why she never pleased the boss. Surely she must be doing something wrong, she thought. I knew her boss and, although I didn't tell Suzanne this, he was widely known as a critical, egotistical know-it-all. There wasn't anything she—or anyone else—could do that would please him. What Suzanne didn't understand was that not all men are like her father, and she couldn't expect them to treat her as he did.

What Suzanne and Carolyn had in common was inappropriately viewing the boss as a father figure. Expecting the best from him, or expecting the worst from him, doesn't allow you to build an independent, objective relationship with your boss or other senior executive.

COACHING TIPS

• If you find yourself responding to the boss or other male authority figures in a way that is unlike you in other situations, ask yourself these three questions:

1. Who does he remind me of?
2. How do I act when I'm around him?
3. Why do I give up so much power to him?

The answers will help you see why and how you see the boss as your father.

• Use self-talk to differentiate male authority figures from your father. When you're in a meeting with the boss, tell yourself he's not your father and you are his equal. Do it as often as needed to believe it and act accordingly.

• Lower your antenna for feelings and focus on the message a male authority figure gives you, not the manner in which it is delivered. This will enable you to hear it objectively and respond appropriately.

ACTION ITEM

Mistake 35

Limiting Your Possibilities

In her book *Women's Reality*, Anne Wilson Schaef observes that in our culture, those with less power live their lives in a zone circumscribed by people with more power. White men, being on the top of the hierarchy, decide what's appropriate behavior for everyone else, including women. In many ways, *Nice Girls Don't Get the Corner Office* is about how women live according to the rules established by men. One obvious example is the Supreme Court. Until only relatively recently—when Sandra Day O'Connor was appointed in 1981—the rules for our entire country were established by men.

Schaef points out that without even realizing it, living our lives this way narrowly circumscribes the choices we make. Like air pollution, if you live in it and breathe it long enough, you come to believe that that's just how the air is supposed to be. It's not until you see the beautiful blue skies of some unspoiled territory that you realize things can be different. For women, the air is polluted all the time, so we don't often have the opportunity to see how things can be different. We come to believe that our possibilities are limited, when in fact they're limited only because we *allow* them to be.

Not too long ago a woman was referred to me because she wanted to explore a career opportunity for which she was qualified but uncertain about tossing her hat in the ring for. For many years she had worked at a nonprofit organization as the second in command. She had seen directors (all male) come and go and never really thought of herself as a contender for the top job. The board of directors was made up exclusively of conservative men, and they had never considered her for the job when the top position became available. This made her believe she would never be considered a viable candidate.

After our first meeting, it was clear to both of us that she had the talent and the experience to do the job; she just didn't have the confidence. She'd grown up in a household where an older brother was the anointed superstar of the family, and she was given the message that she was good, but not nearly as talented as he was. It was pretty clear why, up until now, she was satisfied in positions where she played second fiddle.

At our second meeting I wanted to know why now, after all these years, she wanted the top spot. She said she'd been looking around at women colleagues who had begun their careers in pretty much the same position she had—and they were all now executive directors and presidents of their nonprofit institutions. Part of the shift in thinking was out of embarrassment, and part was because she was bored and ready for a new challenge.

By our third meeting the woman had put together a plan for how she was going to express her interest in the job and show why she was the best-qualified candidate. Within two months (this was a very slow-moving board!) she was the lead contender for the job, and within three months she was sitting in the director's corner office.

In a society where women are given so many subtle and not-so-subtle messages about "where they belong," it's important to think outside the artificially narrowed box. One of the most powerful women in the entertainment industry, if not the most powerful, is the Paramount Pictures CEO, Sherry Lansing. Recognizing that the chance to run her own studio would never be handed to her, Lansing started her own production company. When her company produced such blockbuster films such as *Fatal Attraction* and *The Accused*, the studio heads took note. Within a short period of time she was invited back to play with the big boys and given the top spot at Paramount. The lesson here is: If you live your life within the boundaries circumscribed by others, you'll never know the full scope of your potential—nor will anyone else.

COACHING TIPS

- Consciously expand your world of possibilities by enumerating your choices at every fork in the road. If you can't see them, brainstorm with a friend.
- Listen for limiting self-talk such as:

"I could never do what Kathy did. I'm not that brave."
"They'll never approve of this idea no matter how many facts I present."
"I may as well not even apply for that job. I'm not the best qualified."
"I'm not smart enough to get a Ph.D."
"I'll never have enough money to retire early."

- Avoid the tendency to disregard unconventional choices. Before making a decision about a direction, sleep on all your choices. One that you may initially discount could be the right one for you.
- Read biographies of successful women and learn how they broadened their possibilities.
- Ignore naysayers. People told Mary Kay Ash she couldn't possibly start a successful cosmetics company—and look what she did!

ACTION ITEM

Mistake 36

Ignoring the Quid Pro Quo

*P*eople don't like to talk about it, but inherent to every relationship there's a quid pro quo—something that's exchanged in return for something else. The quid pro quo can be obvious, such as *I give you a salary and in return I expect you to do a good job*, or more subtle, like *I give you a recommendation and in turn expect you'll help me get my expense check processed faster*. It's an unspoken system of bartering that goes on in relationships. Women aren't very good at capitalizing on the quid pro quo. Instead, they give away favors and expect little or nothing in return.

An important part of building relationships at work is identifying the quid pro quo. What do you have that others want or need, and what do others have that you want or need? Every time you give people something they need, a (figurative) chip is deposited in your account. The trick is to always have more chips in your account than you need. The only way you can do this is by interacting with others with generosity of spirit.

It really isn't as manipulative or mercenary as it sounds. We do it all day long without realizing it. Say, for example, that I finish up a report for you because you have to leave early for a doctor's appointment. I collect a chip. Several weeks later I need some information that I know you've collected through your research. I cash that chip in when you give me the information. Sometimes the quid pro quo is verbalized ("Remember when I loaned you my laptop last month? Well, I've got a favor to ask . . ."), but more often it's not.

COACHING TIPS

- When you go out of your way for people, be sure to let them know. A subtle way to do it is to say something like, "Can I finish this report before I leave? Well, I was planning on meeting a friend after work but why don't I call him and let him know I'll be late." You've just collected a chip.

- Don't make things look so easy. Try saying something similar to, "I'm happy to report that I convinced the IT department to repair your laptop ahead of several other requests. I knew you would need it before you left on your trip." There's another chip in your account.

- Don't underestimate the barter value of things like verbally supporting someone in a meeting, public praise, a listening ear, or grapevine information. They're all valuable workplace commodities.

- Cash in your chips sparingly, but don't be afraid to use them. If you're applying for a job and someone you've collected many chips from has information about the hiring source, ask for it. When you need someone to help out in a pinch, ask someone you've extended the same courtesy to in the past. Keep in mind that the exchange of chips isn't always one-to-one, it isn't always immediately following the point of collection, and it doesn't have to be made obvious.

ACTION ITEM

Mistake 37

Skipping Meetings

*L*ose the notion that meetings are supposed to be valuable, interesting, or worth your time. That's really naive. Also lose the inclination to stay at your desk and work because *that's* really important. Wrong again. I realize that most meetings are an incredible waste of time if you think the content is what they're all about. It's not. Meetings are to see and be seen, meet and greet, or play show-and-tell. It's part of the branding and marketing you'll read about in chapter 5—something most women need to do *much* more of.

COACHING TIPS

- Don't skip meetings. (How's that for direct and to the point?)
- Use meetings as an opportunity to showcase a particular skill or piece of knowledge (provided it's not note taking or coffee making). If you're good at facilitating, then offer to lead the meeting (it's much better than sitting there bored). Or if you want to build a relationship, support what someone else says (but only if you really agree with it).
- *Ask* to be invited to meetings where you'll have the chance to meet senior management or make a presentation about something for which you need support.

ACTION ITEM

Mistake 38

Putting Work Ahead of Your Personal Life

*D*on't make work your life. The CEO of one *Fortune* 100 company (a man, of course) told me, "If my staff can't get the job done and have a life outside of work, they're doing something wrong." When all is said and done, do you really want written on your tombstone: SHE ALWAYS PUT THE NEEDS OF THE COMPANY AHEAD OF HER OWN? You owe the company an honest day's work for an honest day's pay. You owe the company a reasonable amount of overtime (with or without pay, but always without complaint). You don't owe the company your soul.

My experience with women who give up what's important to them to meet the needs of the job is that they either don't have anything to go home to or they don't want to deal with what they do have to go home to. Having activities and people outside of work that are important to you helps you remain positive and productive. It's a fallacy that you have to give up your life to have a successful career. All work and no play makes Jill a *very* dull girl.

COACHING TIPS

- Think twice before canceling plans because you're asked to or because you're swamped. Weigh the rewards against the risks involved with doing so. There are legitimately times when you have to cancel, but if these are the rule instead of the exception something's wrong with the picture.
- Never cancel plans with your children because of a workplace request unless your job is on the line. Even then think twice. You obviously can't risk losing a job you need for financial reasons, but you might want to ask yourself if you wouldn't be better off at a company that embraces family values.
- Develop outside hobbies and interests. If you don't have one, *create* a reason for leaving work.
- What *do* you want written on your tombstone? Then do it.

ACTION ITEM

Mistake 39

Letting People Waste Your Time

I just *know* we must have GO AHEAD—WASTE MY DAY written on our foreheads. Why else would people think they could spend so much time talking to us about nothing? I cannot understand why anyone—man, woman, or child—would come into my office and say, "Would you mind if I ask you a question? Bob is busy at the moment." Like *I'm* not? Your time is one of the most precious commodities you have. Once it's gone, you'll never retrieve it.

So we're supposed to be nurturing and kind and blah, blah, blah, blah, blah. Well, I'm here to tell you, being nurturing and kind is not mutually exclusive of being protective of your time. There's a time and place for everything, and when you've got a tight deadline, a five-thirty hairdresser appointment, and your in-laws are coming for dinner—it's *definitely* not the time.

Christine Reiter, president of the Pasadena-based consulting firm Time Strategies, works with clients to maximize the use of their time. When I asked her how women differ from men in terms of time wasters, she told me, "The urge to please everyone and not be able to say no is the biggest time waster for women. We don't like conflict and confrontation. As a result, we have difficulty setting boundaries and making our positions clear."

Don't leave this page thinking my suggestion is that you *never* make time for others. Doing that would only irreparably damage relationships and prevent you from collecting chips that you can later barter. But do think about how you allow others to take advantage of your time, especially when you just don't have it to give.

COACHING TIPS

- Differentiate the times when people *need* to talk from those when they *want* to talk.
- Repeat after me: "You know, I would love to talk more but I'm on a tight schedule today. How about if we continue this conversation tomorrow?"
- Use tricks of time management, like keeping a pile of papers on the extra chairs in your office; not putting your pencil down when someone walks in; answering your phone, voice mail, and e-mail only during specified periods of the day; and putting a PLEASE DO NOT DISTURB sign on your door when you've got a tight deadline.
- A few more tips from Reiter:

1. Clearly set boundaries about how much time you have—or don't have—to share, and know the world will not fall apart because of it.
2. When people ignore the boundary (as they inevitably do with women), enforce it by saying something like, "As I said before, I'd love to spend more time with you but today's schedule won't allow me to."
3. If others keep you waiting more than twenty or thirty minutes for a scheduled appointment, leave. This includes business lunches, doctor's appointments, and casual encounters with friends.

ACTION ITEM

Mistake 40

Prematurely Abandoning Your Career Goals

$\mathcal{S}$uccess breeds success. Eleanor Roosevelt said, "You gain courage and confidence from doing the things you think you cannot do." The problem encountered by many women is that they often allow others to sidetrack them from their early dreams and career goals. Mary Catherine Bateson, daughter of anthropologists Margaret Mead and Gregory Bateson, wrote a wonderfully insightful book titled *Composing a Life*. Her observation is that women's lives, unlike men's, are not linear but rather constantly shifting. "Our lives not only take new directions," she writes, "they are subject to repeated redirection, partly because of the extension of our years of health and productivity." It's this redirection that gets in our way of making plans and pursuing them through to completion. As a result, when we're interested in returning to them, we may find the workforce is no longer interested in us.

When I worked at ARCO I saw numerous well-educated, bright women who were considered only for entry-level positions because they had abandoned their early career goals. They erroneously thought they would be able to pick up their careers where they left off. I once interviewed a woman for a position within corporate communications who had many starts and stops in her career. She had earned a college degree in English, intending to go into the newspaper business as a writer or editor. For the past twelve years she'd held various administrative positions for short periods of time (eight to eighteen months) as she moved around the country with her husband's job changes. She was a lovely woman who was clearly bright but, when asked, admitted she was not up to speed with state-of-the-art office technology and equipment. Combined with a spotty work history, she wasn't someone I could in good conscience further to the next stage of candidacy.

If she had at least kept up to date with technology I would have considered her along with other candidates. If she had achieved any of her personal goals—regardless of how minor they may appear—I would have assessed her as more likely to perseveringly pursue the goals of the communications department. Instead, like many other women in her situation, her best chance of eventually getting the position she wanted would be to begin with an entry-level secretarial position and work her way up.

Even if circumstances prevent you from achieving your goal of being editor in chief of a major metropolitan newspaper, remain involved with your interests and up to date with your field of interest. You may have what it takes to be successful, but if you lose yourself in someone else's priorities or societal expectations you can't be judged by your potential but rather by your history.

COACHING TIPS

- Rather than completely abandon your career goals when life throws you a curve, come up with a strategic life plan that allows you to keep abreast of developments in your field. Talk to friends and family and ask for their support in helping you to remain on your path.

- Consider the importance of a college degree not only to your success, but to your self-confidence, as well. Even if you don't need it for work, do you want it for you? If so, start downloading the application.

- When others attempt to derail you from your path, look at it as normal—but don't give in to it. When any "system" changes, whether it's a political system, an ecological system, or a family system, the system tends to want to maintain its equilibrium by going back to the status quo. So guess what? People are used to the status quo being your putting your needs on a back burner—and if they had their druthers, they'd keep it that way.

- If you decide to be a stay-at-home mom for a while, remain involved with your field through participation in professional associations or community college courses.

- Volunteer to do work in your field of interest that will allow you access to the technology and equipment you will need when you return to work.

ACTION ITEM

Mistake 41

Ignoring the Importance of Network Relationships

*O*nce upon a time, in a decade very far away, people would do their jobs, collect their paycheck, go home, and know that as long as they did their job well, they could sleep easily at night. They would be taken care of. Only in a fairy tale would this scenario be true today. There was a time when IBM was notorious for its full-employment policy. Even during difficult financial times, you wouldn't be laid off. Your hours might be cut or you might be transferred to the boondocks, but IBM founder Tom Watson prided himself on the full-employment policy. Not anymore.

Many women still believe in that fairy tale. They go to work, do a good job, try not to make any waves, and think this is enough to protect them from career derailment. As Judge Judy would say: *"Wrong."* You are in the center of a complex network of people.

CHART 4

NETWORK RELATIONSHIPS

SENIOR MANAGEMENT

YOUR TEAM LEADER

EXTERNAL CLIENTS/ CUSTOMERS

YOUR TEAM LEADER'S COLLEAGUES

INTERNAL CLIENTS/ CUSTOMERS

YOU

INTERNAL COLLEAGUES

VENDORS

INTERNAL COLLEAGUES' STAFF

YOUR STAFF

EXTERNAL PROFESSIONAL COLLEAGUES

Your job includes building a relationship with everyone on that wheel. You don't have to do it on the golf course or over beers after work, but you do have to do it if you want to ensure long-term success.

Rather than share with you a story about a woman whose career was negatively impacted by her failure to maintain network relationships, let me tell you one about a woman whose career was saved by those relationships. Alexis is an executive with responsibility for the North American sales group of an international toy company. After quite a few years working for the company, her boss left and was replaced with someone from outside the firm. Alexis and the new boss didn't see eye-to-eye on many issues, and dissatisfaction on both ends inevitably arose.

The new boss was ready to fire her and asked human resources to help him do so. He admitted she did a fine job, was a hard worker, and always met her sales goals, but they disagreed on some significant changes he wanted to make in the business. To bolster his case, he suggested they conduct a survey of people in her network, asking for feedback about her performance. He assumed that if *he* didn't get along with her, then others must not as well.

Well, was he surprised by the results. It turned out the woman was a superb networker. She built strong relationships not only with customers of the company, but with vendors, coworkers, and people reporting to her also. To a person they praised her for her work ethic, integrity, and attention to customer needs. From reading their comments, you would believe they'd named their first, second, and third children after her. It was pretty clear that if the new boss fired her, he would lose goodwill throughout the company's community of employees and customers. Instead, as a result of her network relationships, he was forced to find a way to work more effectively with her.

The story demonstrates the power of network relationships. Most of us aren't in situations this dramatic, but we all do need to call on relationships every now and then to help us out professionally. And remember: *When you need that relationship, it's already too late to build it.*

COACHING TIPS

- Go back to the network diagram on page 113 and beneath each category write the names of actual people who impact your work and career.
- Develop a plan for how you're going to build (or maintain) a relationship with each of them. Consider the possible quid pro quo (see Mistakes 9 and 36).
- Join and actively participate in a professional association.
- Tell yourself, "Spending time building relationships is not a waste of time." And it's not. The more relationships you have in place, the more access you have to information and resources.
- Keep a notebook or create a database that includes all the people you meet and the information they shared with you.

ACTION ITEM

Mistake 42

Refusing Perks

*T*oni was promoted to a senior management position in her firm. The company, like many others, had a policy about which levels of employee were entitled to which offices. You know the story— those on the bottom of the food chain get an inside cubicle, next up get a cubicle with a window, next up a double-sized cubicle, and so on up to a corner office, with a door, mahogany furniture, and a predetermined color of carpet. (When I worked in corporate America, I used to say, "I want to be promoted to a *door*.") Toni was entitled to an office, with a window (and a door) and faux mahogany furniture. When she was informed it was time to move from her double-sized cubicle with a window, she refused. She didn't see the need to go to the trouble and expense to move. Mistake!

Nancy experienced a similar situation. Due to a promotion, she was entitled to a new office, furniture, PC, and so on. In her case, Nancy expected to move into her new space and was waiting for the green light to do so—but the green light never came. One day she went to her boss and asked what was up. He informed her that he'd recently hired someone for whom he would need the office she'd expected. You guessed it: The new hire was a man. Rather than make waves, Nancy stayed in her cubicle, grateful for even being promoted. Even bigger mistake!

COACHING TIPS

- You don't take a perk because you want it, or think you deserve it. You take it because it manages the impressions others have of you—and those you have of yourself.

- When a perk you've earned is—shall we say—"overlooked," bring it to management's attention. It could legitimately be an oversight. Then again, they could just be hoping you act like most women and never bring it up.

- When you're not given perks commensurate with your position, and you know it's not an oversight, ask why not. At a minimum, make someone look you in the eye and tell you why you're not getting what everyone else in your position gets.

- If you feel strongly about the slight and are willing to accept the consequences, bring the matter to senior management for a final decision. Without being whiny or pointing fingers, explain the situation, what you would like to have happen, and in what time frame. The worst you will hear is no, in which case you let it go unless it's the hill you're willing to die on.

- When you get a promotion, be sure to ask what it includes. Often information either doesn't flow automatically or is delayed.

ACTION ITEM

Mistake 43

Making Up Negative Stories

$\mathcal{M}$y mother was a master at making up negative stories when things went wrong. If someone was a bit cool to her, she would think out loud, "Maybe the gift I gave him wasn't nice enough." If I didn't get a particular job, it was, "Maybe you didn't wear the right dress." If my father didn't get a promotion, he heard, "Maybe you insulted the boss." As a result, whenever things didn't go quite as I had planned, I assumed I'd done something wrong—and I know I'm not alone. Many women suffer from this same phenomenon, and for the same reason!

At work, making up negative stories will serve to continually put you in a position of having to second-guess yourself or, worse yet, being hesitant to take risks for fear of something coming back to haunt you. It can also be immobilizing.

Let me give you an example. A former client called to discuss a promotional opportunity being offered to her. She would be moving from an individual contributor to manager of her department. Since she had been with her firm for a relatively short period of time, it was quite a compliment to be offered this position. Within hours of being offered the job, however, she had made up so many negative stories about what could go wrong that she became hesitant to accept the assignment for fear of failing at it.

It wasn't that she was wrong in her diagnosis about the potential pitfalls; it was that she couldn't overcome this negative thinking long enough to find the many ways there were to obviate them. Had she not been capable of handling the challenges inherent to the position, she never would have been offered it in the first place. She did wind up accepting the position, and (to no one's surprise except perhaps her own) she's doing beautifully.

COACHING TIPS

- To begin, replace negative stories with more neutral ones. Consider alternative scenarios that could explain what has happened that have nothing to do with *you* doing something wrong.
- Focus on solutions to problems, not the problems themselves. Wallowing in a sea of negativity will cause you to miss the obvious solutions.
- Read *Feel the Fear and Do It Anyway*, by Susan Jeffers. This one is an oldie but goodie. As the title suggests, you can't let fear get in your way of going for the gold. The book offers concrete suggestions for how to turn negative thinking into positive results.

ACTION ITEM

Mistake 44

Striving for Perfection

*H*aving been made to believe we're totally flawed, imperfect beings, women overcompensate by striving for perfection. Intellectually we know it's impossible, but emotionally we go there every time we feel insecure or less than competent. What a waste of time and energy! We would be much better off using the time we spend perfecting already good work products or relationships on new and creative endeavors. Elsewhere in this book I talk about how we allow *others* to waste our time. Well, this is one way in which we waste our *own* time.

Julia is the perfect example. Before she came for coaching, she would drive herself crazy checking and rechecking—then checking one more time—everything that left her office. Her compulsion around perfection caused her marriage to fail, created physical problems for her, and made the people who worked with her absolutely nuts. No one wanted to have her on their team because she was known for being so nitpicky. Her career was severely limited by her inability to let go of the small stuff. She unintentionally conveyed the message to others that nothing was good enough for her. She made them feel as if *they* weren't good enough. Who wants to work with or for someone like that?

COACHING TIPS

- Consciously reduce the amount of time you work on any given day or spend on any one piece of work. If you know you have only one hour to proof a report, then you'll do it in an hour. If you leave the schedule open-ended, perfection-seeking behavior will result in your putting in more hours at work than necessary.
- Ask for feedback. Before putting in extra time on what might already be a completed product, ask a colleague what he or she thinks. It may be that it's perfectly fine as is.
- If your behavior borders on obsessive or compulsive, consider seeking professional help for the purpose of assessing whether medication could be helpful in soothing the anxiety often associated with being perfectionistic.
- Strive for 80 percent perfection. The difference between 80 percent and 100 percent won't be noticed by most people but will buy you more time to shift to other important tasks.
- Ask yourself often, "Is this a valuable use of my time?" If the answer is yes, ask yourself, "Why?" If your answer is tied to your self-image and what people will think of you, you may be guilty of striving for perfection.
- Relinquish the need to be seen as perfect and settle for being viewed as human. After all, you are a human *being*, not a human *doing*.

ACTION ITEM ☐

Chapter 5

How You Brand and Market Yourself

When you think about well-known name brands, which ones come to mind? If you're like most people, names like *Kleenex, Coke,* and *Xerox* immediately pop up. Not only are the names familiar, but they've also become synonymous with the product. When we go to a restaurant and ask for a Coke, we may or may not be served a drink made by Coca-Cola. We make Xerox copies, regardless of the actual machine being used. "Hand me a Kleenex" doesn't necessarily mean Kleenex brand. Brand names get a good reputation as a result of two things: consistent quality and marketing. One without the other doesn't equate to staying power or success in the marketplace.

Dr. Bruce Heller, president of Strategic Leadership Solutions in Encino, California, coaches professionals about the importance of thinking of themselves as brands to be marketed. "You have to look at the workplace as a marketplace," Heller says. "In this market, your product is *you*." You create a brand for yourself by first identifying what distinguishes you from other people in the workplace and then marketing those distinctions as a brand.

One of Dr. Heller's favorite phrases—*Outta sight, outta mind, outta business*—is particularly important for women to remember. As young girls we often learn that we are to be seen but not heard. Carrying that forward to adulthood translates into doing our work in a quiet and unassuming way. I often hear women say they don't care if they're given credit; they're just happy to make a contribution to the bottom line. The result is that we are overlooked for promotions and assignments we've actually earned and deserve. The coaching tips in the next section are designed to help you define your brand, acknowledge the value of your brand, and develop a plan for marketing your brand.

Mistake 45

Failing to Define Your Brand

*N*ot too long ago I interviewed a woman with a doctorate in organization development for a vacancy on our coaching team. Her résumé was impressive. She seemed to have the kind of experience and education I sought, but I wasn't sure of her specialty area. Because we're known as a firm with subject-matter experts who can provide executives with unique expertise in their areas for development, one of the first questions I posed to this woman was, "Tell me about what you're best known for." For the next thirty-five minutes she told me all about what she had done, what her interests were, and the many ways in which she could add value. The problem was, she didn't answer my question. Despite another forty-five minutes of probing and asking the question in several different ways, I never learned what made her unique among all organizational psychologists.

Peter Montoya is the publisher of a magazine called *Personal Branding.* In the first issue he wrote, "A personal brand is a promise of performance that creates expectations in its audience. Done well, it clearly communicates the values, personality, and abilities of the person behind it." That's what was missing from my interview with the woman who wanted to be on our coaching team—

but wasn't selected because of her inability to clearly define her brand for me.

COACHING TIPS

- Make a list of the three to five things that bring you the most satisfaction at work. We tend to be good at what we like, so focusing first on these will help to point you in the right direction. You might come up with responses such as *help others, listen, problem solve, negotiate, write technical reports, manage projects, collect data, identify obstacles, implement solutions,* and more.
- Next, translate these behaviors into three key strengths you bring to your workplace. For example, "My ability to listen effectively enables me to gather data from reluctant sources. Tied in with that is skill at writing, which allows me to report that data in an objective way. Third, once the data is collected and reported, I've exhibited the ability to identify and implement solutions to problems." Practice saying these words out loud so that when the time is right you can recite them fluently and confidently.
- Consider how these behaviors distinguish you from others. For example, the ability to gather and report data may be unique in a department or company mainly known for producing a product. Or having skill in building relationships may be unique and valuable in an organization where intellectual capital is the product.

ACTION ITEM

Mistake 46

Minimizing Your Work or Position

I can't tell you how many times I've heard women respond to the question, "What do you do?" with a self-deprecating answer. "Oh, I *just* manage a legal office." "I'm *only* an administrative assistant." "I *kind of* run the information technology group." These comments don't sound like brands I would be interested in learning more about. Instead, they reveal a feeling of embarrassment or lack of pride in what the person does. *Every* job in *every* organization is critical to its operation. You may not be the president of IBM, but you wouldn't have your job if it wasn't necessary to run the business. Identifying why your business needs *you* is crucial to accurately marketing your brand.

Related to this is the ability to *succinctly* tell others what you do while putting the most positive spin possible on your statement. I'm not saying *lie*, but I am saying you should express pride at the way in which you help your organization succeed at reaching its business objectives. If you can't tell someone during an elevator ride (in a short building) what you do, then you haven't finished defining your brand.

COACHING TIPS

• Hone your elevator speech. Make it brief, void of minimizing words, and inclusive of your strengths. For example:

"I'm the project coordinator for an architectural firm. My job is to ensure the success of our business through timely delivery of our high-quality services."

"I work for a trucking firm where my responsibility is to accurately code parcels that are sure to reach their destination in the quickest time possible."

"As the manager of a team of five salespeople, I motivate and coach the staff to achieve higher-than-expected sales."

"At the current time I'm seeking a position that will utilize nearly ten years' experience in writing technical manuals that ensure the safe and efficient operation of laboratory equipment."

• Consider couching your achievements using the PAR model: Problem–Action–Results. For example: "I identify problems with system efficiencies and recommend remedies that result in cost savings to the company."

ACTION ITEM ☐

Mistake 47

Using Only Your Nickname or First Name

*W*hen was the last time you heard a male executive called by the diminutive of his name? *Billy Gates. Jackie Welch. Sammy Walton.* I don't think so. The diminutive of *anything* diminishes its importance. All nicknames and diminutives are used as a fond way of referring to children. As adults, it serves the same purpose—but most men drop it by the time they're teenagers. Laura Bush may have been able to call the president *Georgie*, but you wouldn't catch any of his aides getting away with it.

I've also been amazed to watch women introduce themselves using their formal name, only to have the person immediately shorten it. A client of mine named Teresa tells me that within moments of introducing herself, she's called *Terri*. "I never heard anyone change Jim to Jimmy," she says.

Similarly, whenever I hear a woman answer the phone with only her first name, or leave a voice-mail message that says, "This is Sarah. Please leave your message . . . ," it makes me wonder why she dropped her last name. It's common among administrative staff—and entirely unnecessary. You will rarely hear a man answer the phone using only his first name. It's a small but significant difference. Using only your first name relegates you, once again, to a childlike status. Ask a child his or her name and most often you get only the first name. The combination of your first and last names moves you to adulthood.

COACHING TIPS

- Even if you've gone by *Kathy, Debbie, Maggie,* or *Sandy* your entire life, begin introducing yourself using your formal name. Over time, people will take your cue. Change your business cards, desk nameplate, or formal letterhead to read *Kathleen, Debra, Margaret,* or *Sandra.* You'll be much more likely to be taken seriously if you don't use your childhood nickname for professional purposes.

- Always use your first and last name on your voice-mail message, in your e-mail address, when introducing yourself, and when answering the phone.

- If people change your name to the diminutive, correct them by simply repeating the name you prefer them to use.

ACTION ITEM

Mistake 48

Waiting to Be Noticed

$\mathcal{D}$uring a recent downsizing in her corporation, Jacqueline desperately wanted to stay on in either her current position or another one. She knew that behind closed doors, decisions were being made about who would stay and who would go. While she waited nervously to be told her fate, I suggested she had nothing to lose by going to her boss and human resource representative to make a case for staying. It was as if I'd suggested she race nude across the executive floor. Not only couldn't she fathom coming up with something to say that could possibly make a difference, she couldn't picture herself going in and saying it.

Corporate downsizings and the trend toward flat organizations have created the need to be noticed in a positive way—*before* workforce reductions take place. When it comes to maintaining your job during layoffs, it can be as simple as making a case for why your unique brand will be valuable in the newly formed organization.

As for flatter organizations, the dearth of opportunities to move *up* makes assignments and projects that can offer you visibility or specialized training all the more valuable. Recipients of these assignments are often those who subtly (and at times not-so-subtly) call attention to the ways in which their strengths play to the requirements of the work. Waiting to be noticed will not get you where you want to be. You've got to know your brand and sell it when the opportunity arises. Women, especially those who are not particularly good at "selling" themselves, are often overlooked—not because of lack of capability, but because of modesty or the mistaken belief that their accomplishments will eventually be noticed.

COACHING TIPS

- If there's a vacancy or assignment you want, *ask* to be considered for it.
- When you're ready to make a career move, *talk about it out loud*. Let people know you're ready for the next challenge. The more people you talk to about it, the more likely you are to hear about opportunities when they arise.
- *Continually* showcase your achievements in subtle ways. One suggestion is to prepare a weekly or biweekly status sheet listing your accomplishments or those of your department. Another is to share your achievements in the form of "best practices." For example, at a staff meeting you could share with your colleagues how you solved a particular problem or overcame an obstacle that threatened a deadline.
- Develop a marketing plan. Envision your future and *write down the specific steps* you'll take to get there.
- Spend time engaged in learning, soliciting feedback or getting coaching, and doing something different than what you're already good at. These three things prepare you for unexpected challenges and opportunities.

ACTION ITEM

Mistake 49

Refusing High-Profile Assignments

$\mathcal{T}$he director of operations at a small East Coast branch of a manufacturing firm headquartered in Los Angeles was asked to sit on the executive committee of her company. She had long complained that she wasn't recognized for her achievements in turning around what had been a money-losing operation. The request to sit on the EC made a strong statement about not only her value to her own division, but also the contributions she could make throughout the firm. And what did she do? *She turned it down* because in the past she had attended several of their meetings and saw them as "a waste of time." The first words out of my mouth were, "Quit bein' a girl!" I couldn't help myself. Without considering the bigger picture, she acted in a manner consistent with the values she'd learned in childhood—to work hard and not waste the company's time or money.

The opportunity to showcase your capabilities through a high-profile assignment isn't limited to something as grand as being invited to sit on your company's executive committee. Being asked to facilitate an important meeting, to make a critical client presentation, or to make a presentation to your senior management are all examples of high-profile assignments you can't afford to pass up.

I understand that we're all oversubscribed, that meetings can go on for what seems like an eternity, and that making client presentations can be a lot of work and a little risky. So what? Use these opportunities to profile your unique capabilities and build relationships with others who are viewed as movers and shakers. Remember, 90 percent of success comes from just showing up!

COACHING TIPS

- When you're asked to sit at the table, graciously accept the invitation. If you don't have the time, make the time. It's an investment in your future.
- When offered a position or assignment that's new to you, *take it*. If others have enough confidence in you that you can do the job, *you should, too*.
- Request potentially risky but high-profile projects. No guts, no glory.
- Volunteer to give presentations to senior management. The benefits typically outweigh the risks and you can't get comfortable doing it unless you do it. Exposure to senior management is critical for recognition.
- Keep in mind that in the workplace, senior executives are your customers. Therefore, you need to be in situations where you can identify their needs and serve them.

ACTION ITEM ☐

Mistake 50

Being Modest

$\mathcal{B}$oth boys and girls are taught in childhood to be modest—but women take the lesson *way* too far. There's a time and place for modesty. When you've moved a mountain, broken the sound barrier, or produced a miracle, it's neither the time nor place. When people fail to notice major accomplishments, *it's your job* to illuminate them. Making things look easy or seamless when in fact they required Herculean efforts isn't a great marketing technique.

Helena provides a great example of being much too modest. As director of executive development, she and her team are responsible for performing management assessments, designing individualized development programs for each top member of management, and providing executive coaching. When her company merged with another firm, the size of her job nearly doubled, yet the size of her team remained the same. Nonetheless, she found creative ways to get the job done with the people available to her.

During her annual performance review, Helena's boss commended her for the extra effort she put in and gave her a generous bonus. Pleased that he'd recognized her good work, she modestly responded, "It really wasn't anything." She had gone into the meeting wanting to bring up the need for additional staff, but when he complimented her and gave her the bonus, she was completely thrown off kilter and failed to parlay his recognition into a marketing opportunity. As a result of her modesty, she had to come up with another strategy for requesting more head count since getting the job done "really wasn't anything."

COACHING TIPS

- Completely, totally, and permanently erase the phrase *Oh—it was nothing* from your vocabulary.
- When reporting accomplishments, give them the import they deserve. Helena should have said something like, "It took everyone on the team working long hours and weekends, but I'm proud of what we did and glad you appreciate it."
- When given a compliment, look the person in the eye and respond with a simple, "Thank you." Avoid downplaying your efforts.
- Forward notes of appreciation or acknowledgment about your work to your manager.
- Prominently display awards or plaques.
- Keep an "atta gal" file—a collection of accomplishments of which you are proud: thank-you notes, outstanding performance reviews, and the like. Review it at those moments when you begin to doubt yourself.

ACTION ITEM

Mistake 51

Staying in Your Safety Zone

I once asked a man why he'd applied for a particular position when he knew he did not meet the stated requirements. His reply was simple: "I'm smart. I'll learn them." Women tend to remain in positions too long for fear of getting in over their heads. Unless a woman is 100 percent confident she meets all of the expectations for the job, she won't consider throwing her hat in the ring. Men are more likely than women to seek stretch assignments—ones they've never done before but want to prove they can.

In the modern job market we look at people who stay in a job *too* long in the same way we used to judge job-hoppers—as if there's something wrong with them. Staying in a job too long gives the impression of being complacent and, perhaps, not staying up on the latest technical developments in the field. Women even refuse assignments for which they are handpicked if they feel they're not qualified for the job. *Big* mistake. There's no surer way to be crossed off the list for future opportunities than by refusing an offer—and there's no greater burden than a good opportunity.

Ironically, even people who stay in their comfort zones aren't attracted or impressed by other people who do the same. Most folks consider those who are enthusiastic, take risks, and exhibit a can-do attitude as charismatic or people they would like to emulate.

COACHING TIPS

- Unless the responsibilities within a particular job change significantly, look for a new assignment about every three years—five years maximum.
- Don't let your fear of failure cause you to overlook jobs you could do with minimal training.
- Stay up on developments in your field by taking classes or reading books. If you haven't learned anything new lately, you're not growing.
- Volunteer for assignments that stretch your skill set or enable you to learn entirely new ones that will flesh out your portfolio. If you're willing to take the calculated risk of possibly failing, it's not selfish to learn on the job.
- Start looking for your next job the day you start a new one. You may not actually make a move for several years, but being open to the possibilities creates a proactive, preemptive focus in the job market.

ACTION ITEM

Mistake 52

Giving Away Your Ideas

This story is all too common. Woman has idea. Woman expresses idea. Idea gets ignored. Man expresses same idea. Man gets promoted. Who's to blame? Woman. She let her idea be stolen instead of calling attention to the source. Why? Because she's unsure of herself to begin with and doesn't want to appear selfish, territorial, confrontational, or not a team player. Every time you give away an idea, you give away a little of your self-respect. Do this enough times and your self-confidence begins to dwindle immeasurably.

Don't make the mistake of assuming your idea is overlooked because you're a woman. I've observed meetings at which women's ideas were ignored for the simplest of reasons: perhaps they didn't speak loudly enough to be heard, or they whispered their concept to the man sitting next to them and he offered it as his own, or the timing was wrong. These are factors you can address fairly easily and unobtrusively.

It's not only about not giving your ideas away, it's also about finding ways to sell them. Your ideas have value in the marketplace called work. Each time you make a suggestion that's actually implemented, you've made a sale. Make enough of these sales and you've collected more of those invisible chips that can later be subtly bartered for favors, plum assignments, or perks.

COACHING TIPS

- Get in the habit of asking a question after expressing an idea. Try something like, "My recommendation is that we prioritize our solutions and select the top two for immediate implementation. Are there any objections to getting to work on this immediately?" This increases the likelihood of acknowledgment and discussion.
- When someone proposes the same thing you previously suggested (albeit in a slightly different way), call attention to the fact by saying, "It sounds like you're building on my original suggestion, and I would certainly support that."
- Speak loudly enough to be heard.
- Rather than seeking affirmation by whispering your idea to the person next to you, take the risk of putting it out directly and confidently.
- Whenever possible or appropriate, put your ideas in writing. It gives them a kind of credibility that just the spoken word lacks, and reminds people where the ideas came from. The written word is still one of the most powerful forms of communication, and some people respond much more favorably if they can "see" what you're saying.

ACTION ITEM

Mistake 53

Working in Stereotypical Roles or Departments

*F*or more than twenty years I've watched women in stereotypical roles—administrative assistants, personnel department staffers, clerks—go to school at night and earn college degrees in the hope of moving up the corporate ladder. I've also seen women with degrees enter the workforce in stereotypically female roles as a strategy to get their foot in the door in the hope of being noticed and promoted. Unfortunately, I haven't seen many who were successful in either scenario. Spending time in a "female ghetto" makes you more likely to be branded as unworthy of a senior assignment. Do I think this is right? Of course not.

Look around your company. Are there departments in your organization like this? Human resources and personnel often fall into this category. The fact that there are more women nurses than male and more women grammar school teachers than male has traditionally caused pay in these areas to be less than the work warrants.

Are you in one of these situations? If so, your status will not be viewed on a par with people working in departments where men and women are represented in essentially equal numbers. A good example of this is found in the banking industry. When tellers were predominantly men, the position was considered somewhat prestigious. As more and more women filled these roles, the pay scale for tellers declined and the position lost its glitter. Remaining too long in such a role or department will eventually limit your marketability.

COACHING TIPS

- Seek assignments in departments or fields where there are comparable numbers of men and women.
- When asked to take a stereotypical role, consider whether the long-term benefits outweigh the short-term ones.
- Never volunteer to make coffee or copies for a meeting. If asked, suggest the responsibility be rotated or assigned based on seniority. (Also see Mistake 89.)
- If moving out of a stereotypical role requires additional training or education, *get it*. It's worth the investment in your future.
- If you acquire the training needed to move out of a stereotypical role and it fails to yield results, consider the possibility you've been "typed" and might need to seek a new organization.

ACTION ITEM

Mistake 54

Ignoring Feedback

*T*here's a word on the street about all of us. It's what people say behind our backs or when we leave a room. You have to know what that is or you can't effectively market yourself. All too often people respond to feedback by either ignoring it (and hoping it will go away) or brushing it off with, "That's just one person's opinion." Perception is reality. People do not know you by your intentions; they know you by your behavior. You can explain or justify your behavior, but it doesn't solve the problem of having a brand that doesn't meet customers' expectations. Sooner or later, people stop buying it. As we tell our clients: "When three people say you're drunk—lie down."

COACHING TIPS

- Ask your human resource department to conduct a 360-degree feedback assessment. This will allow you to see yourself as others see you and provide the opportunity to work on areas for improvement.
- Make it easy for your boss to give you feedback by regularly asking for it.
- When given feedback, respond with a nondefensive inquiry: "Can you tell me more about how and when I do that?" Avoid responding with explanations for how and why you do it.
- When the feedback stings, ask for time to think about it. If you need clarification, get back to the person and ask for it when you can do so unemotionally.
- Most people are reluctant to give honest feedback so, when you get it, consider it a gift.
- If you ask for feedback, it implies that you're going to do something with it. Let people know what you're doing to address your development areas. It calls their attention to any changes you actually make.

ACTION ITEM ☐

Mistake 55

Being Invisible

A young woman was contacted by her college and told she'd been selected as one of several class valedictorians. During this same conversation it was mentioned that she might be called on to make a valedictory address, to which she replied, "Oh, I hope not." Even though she was honored by the thought, like many women she wanted to remain invisible. I see the same behavior among women in the workplace. When people are sought to make presentations to senior management, women are far more reluctant than men to volunteer for the assignment and, when selected without offering, often defer to a male colleague.

I facilitate a leadership program (for men and women) in which participants from the same company work in small groups to solve a real-world problem faced by their firm. Using a specified problem-solving model, they are asked to come up with a solution that includes problem identification, causes, and recommendations for overcoming it, as well as the preparation of a presentation for senior management. On the last day of the program, senior executives from the company are invited to listen to the presentations and comment on the viability of what is suggested. Many times the end product is so good that the proposed solutions are incorporated into the company's business plan.

Inevitably, the women in the program are the worker bees in this exercise. They keep the guys focused; they prepare the overheads or PowerPoint slides for the presentation; they ensure everyone's opinion is heard and taken into consideration. When it comes to who will lead the presentation, it's entirely another story. In nearly twenty years of doing this particular exercise, I can't recall one time when a woman took the lead. Instead, they suggested that the most verbal man lead the presentation team.

Women are invisible enough without having to take extra steps to be doubly certain they aren't seen or noticed! These situations present the perfect opportunities to market your brand. Don't hand it over to a competitor—even if it is friendly competition.

COACHING TIPS

- Volunteer to chair regular department meetings.
- Submit a proposal to make a presentation in your area of expertise at a professional association meeting.
- Write articles for local newspapers, professional journals, or your company newsletter.
- When volunteers are asked to speak to senior management, seize the opportunity.
- In meetings, make certain you don't remain invisible. Voicing your ideas is a great way to market your brand.

ACTION ITEM

Chapter 6

How You Sound

There's a Chinese curse that afflicts many women: *May you have a wonderful idea and not be able to convince anyone of it.* The best ideas fall on deaf ears if they're not communicated in ways that instill confidence and credibility. *How you sound* doesn't refer to the content of your messages but rather to your word choices, tone of voice, speed of speech, and how you organize your thoughts. Each of these factors contributes to whether you are viewed as a knowledgeable, self-confident, and competent professional.

This next section examines each of these factors and gives you specific language to practice. Try saying some of the Coaching Tips out loud to get a feel for how they might sound. Avoid the inclination to discard a tip just because it feels uncomfortable or awkward—it may be the one you need most. Remember, combined with how you look, how you sound comprises more than 90 percent of the perception of your credibility.

Mistake 56

Couching Statements as Questions

*T*his is the most common mistake I hear women make: asking a question as a safe way of expressing an idea without being perceived as too direct or pushy. Such questions typically take the form of, "What would you think if we . . . ?" or "Have you considered . . . ?" By asking a question rather than making a statement, we relinquish ownership of and the outcomes for our ideas. Consider this exchange:

ANN: Do you think we should budget more money for development this year so that we can meet unexpected but emerging needs?

PETE: No. I think we should put more money into marketing. We first need to create buzz and then worry about filling the need.

ANN: That's true, but we have to be prepared to fill the need upon demand, and that requires development funds.

PETE: So why'd you ask me?

If you ask a question to camouflage a statement, it's a little like trying to teach a pig to sing—it frustrates you and annoys the pig. If you're worried about sounding too strident or pushy, consider adding language to the message that would make it more palatable—but at all costs avoid turning it into a question.

COACHING TIPS

- Start making statements. Each time you find yourself couching an opinion in the form of a question, stop and turn it into a statement.
- Save your questions for those times when you *legitimately* need information or are interested in someone's opinion.
- Put ideas out in the affirmative: "I propose we prepare ourselves for emerging needs by putting the bulk of our budget moneys into development." Even if someone disagrees with you, it leaves you in a much stronger position to defend your proposal.
- Adding "I'm interested in your thoughts" after a proposal or statement can make you more comfortable with being direct without making you appear uncertain.

ACTION ITEM

Mistake 57

Using Preambles

A preamble is a concoction of words and nonwords used before getting to the main point. It's like a closet filled with clutter. When there's too much clutter, you can't see what's in the closet. The same is true with words. The more words you use, the more diffused your message becomes and the less likely it is the listener will hear your unique message.

Women use preambles as a means of softening their messages for fear of being perceived as too direct or aggressive. What's your response to this preamble?

> You know, I was thinking about this problem we're having with productivity. In fact, I've been talking to other people about it, too. A lot of us share the same concerns over reduced productivity during the last three quarters, so I'm not alone in this. Come to think of it, it might be even more than just those three quarters. It's something we've known about for a long time but haven't measured. At any rate, we've all been trying to find a way to address it and I think I may have come up with an idea. I'm not saying it's the best idea or the only idea—just that it's one idea. In fact, other people have ideas, too, but I'll leave it up to them to share those with you. Now, my idea involves . . .

And the point is . . . ? This person's motto must be, *Why use fewer words when I can use more?* This same message could have been delivered powerfully and confidently using 75 percent fewer words:

> Productivity has been an issue we've struggled with for some time now and I have a proposal for addressing it.

COACHING TIPS

• Give your bottom line first. Organize your thoughts before you open your mouth by asking yourself two simple questions: *What's my main topic?* and *What two or three points do I want the listener to consider?*

• Let your mantra be: *Short sounds confident.* If the message is an important one, practice before delivering it. Hone it using as few words as possible.

• Try combining affirmative declarations with short messages: "I propose we conduct a cross-functional analysis to determine the causes of and cures for reduced productivity during the last three to four quarters."

ACTION ITEM

Mistake 58

Explaining

*T*he counterpoint to the preamble is the lengthy explanation. You *finally* make your point—then you undermine it with an even longer explanation that causes others to mentally check out. Preambles, combined with explanations, are lethal. Why do women pair these fatal flaws more than men? There are a few reasons. More words soften a message, and heaven forbid we sound too powerful. Another is that we fear we haven't been thorough or complete enough, so in an effort to be "perfect" we keep talking. A third reason is that our statements frequently are not acknowledged, so we continue talking in an effort to get feedback. And finally, we overcompensate for our insecurity. We think the more we talk the better case we make . . . when in fact the *opposite* is true.

Let's pick up the preamble from Mistake 57 and pair it with this lengthy explanation:

> . . . I'm not saying it's the best idea or the only idea—just that it's one idea. In fact, other people have ideas, too, but I'll leave it up to them to share those with you. Now, my idea involves doing some kind of a climate survey. You know, the kind where we go out to the employees and ask them questions about their processes, job satisfaction, relationships with their supervisors, and so on. A lot of companies are doing this now. We can either use an outside consultant or our own staff. If it's all right with you, I would be willing to look into what the best way to accomplish this would be. Or if you prefer, you can name a task force to investigate options. On the other hand, if you want I will investigate the options and get back to you.

As I said . . . *lethal.*

COACHING TIPS

- Shorten your explanations by 50 to 75 percent.
- Once you've gotten to the point, follow it up with no more than two or three pieces of supporting information. Then stop. If it's acknowledgment you want, your silence will be the cue for folks to say something.
- Here's what the entire message would sound like if you used all the coaching tips:

> I propose we conduct a cross-functional analysis to determine the causes of and cures for reduced productivity during the last three to four quarters. The results will tell us where our greatest strengths lie, what mistakes we're currently making, and where we should go from here. I'll take the lead on this. Is there anything you would add?

- Resist the internal message that says, *Incomplete*. Saying everything you know related to a topic isn't necessary. Depending on your level of expertise, it may be incomplete to you, but not to the other person. This is a case where less is more.

ACTION ITEM

Mistake 59

Asking Permission

*H*ave you ever noticed that men don't ask for permission? They ask for forgiveness. My hunch is that women ask permission more out of habit than from really needing someone to give them the green light. It's a variation on asking questions to play it safe—but potentially more self-defeating. In our society we expect children, not adults, to ask permission. Every time a woman asks permission to do or say something, she diminishes her stature and relegates herself to the position of a child. She also sets herself up to hear "No." By seeking permission before acting, we are less likely to be accused of making a mistake—but we're also less likely to be viewed as confident risk takers.

Women ask permission for things as simple as taking a day off and as ridiculous as whether they can spend money on a particular service required by the department—despite the fact they have already been given signing authority. I'll never forget a woman who complained to me that she was denied permission for a one-day off-site for her staff while a male coworker took his team on a boondoggle to a local resort for three days. When I inquired as to how she went about making the plans, she admitted she thought she was being politically correct by asking the boss if it would be all right to have everyone gone for a day; his reply was that he preferred this didn't happen. She then went to her coworker and asked him how he'd gotten the boss's approval; he said, "It never occurred to me to ask."

Regardless of your position, you're entitled to take independent action within a given set of boundaries. Your job is to identify those boundaries, clarify them with your boss, and act within them. From administrative assistants to department managers, I observe many who won't make a move without first getting permission. Believe me, your boss wants you to take the ball and run with it. It's what you're paid for, and it makes his or her job infinitely easier.

COACHING TIPS

- *Inform* others of your intentions; don't ask for permission. By informing others you show respect for their need to know, but without *your* action being contingent upon *their* approval.
- Assume equality.
- Turn this:

Would it be all right with you if I work at home tomorrow? I'm expecting a delivery midday.

Into this:

I just wanted to let you know I'll be working at home tomorrow. I've got a delivery coming.

- You can assume that if people have a problem with what you're saying, they'll let you know. From there you can then negotiate from a position of greater strength.
- If using affirmative declarations is difficult for you, soften your message with a follow-up phrase. Rather than asking for permission, try something like this: "I plan to prepare a position paper to address each of the concerns of our client. When it's complete, I'd like to get your input before sharing it with the client."
- Similarly, don't fall into the trap of responding to statements posed as questions. You'll wind up in a spitting match.
- A legitimate question is one in which you are asking for information you don't have or don't know. By all means ask these types of questions, but avoid holding a group hostage with your questions. Be aware of the body language of others that suggests they're ready to move on. Ask additional questions off-line.

ACTION ITEM ☐

Mistake 60

Apologizing

$\mathcal{I}$ was watching the British Open just after Tiger Woods had lost the tournament. The sportscaster interviewing him expressed sympathy for an obviously bad day in which he'd missed some easy shots and just hadn't played up to his normal standard. His response was, "I didn't play poorly. The wind and the conditions were just against me today." It was a reminder of how even in the face of obvious errors and poor performance, men will deny or minimize the mistake rather than assume responsibility or apologize.

Women can take a lesson from this. Apologizing for unintentional, low-profile, nonegregious errors erodes our self-confidence and, in turn, the confidence others have in us. Whether it's inadvertently bumping into someone on the street or making a small mistake in the office, a woman is far more likely to apologize than a man. It's second nature to us and often done in place of confronting the real source of the mistake—the other person's poor communication. It's a conflict-reducing technique, but one that makes you look like you're at fault when in fact you're not.

Here's an example. A woman opened a coaching session by telling me that her boss had just finished berating her over the fact she hadn't informed him of some meeting she'd attended that he wanted to attend as well. The fact was, she had forwarded to him an e-mail with the information about the meeting, but he'd either failed to read it or forgotten to mark it on his calendar. When asked how she handled the situation, I could tell she was proud of her response. Because we happened to have previously talked about the phenomenon of women apologizing, she knew she didn't want to do that. Instead, she very politely told him, "I forwarded the e-mail to you the same day I received the information. If you're saying that in the future you would like me to check with you to be certain you receive information such as this, I'll be happy to."

This was a great response for a number of reasons. First, she didn't fall into the trap of apologizing. She reported that by not doing so she felt far more empowered and less like a child who was being scolded. Second, is there a boss anywhere who wants employees marching into his or her office to confirm receipt of a bunch of e-mails? By thinking on her feet, she came up with an alternative she knew he wasn't going to go for. Essentially, in a very diplomatic way, she put the onus on him to read his mail.

COACHING TIPS

• Start counting the number of times you apologize unnecessarily. Consciously reduce this number by saving your apologies for big-time mistakes (and there aren't many of those).

• When you do make a mistake worth apologizing for, do so only once, then move into a problem-solving mode.

• Turn the inclination to apologize into an objective assessment of what went wrong and ways to fix it.

• Combine the previous coaching tips with an unapologetic statement such as, "Based on the information initially provided to me, I had no idea that was your expectation. Tell me more about what you had in mind and I'll make the necessary revisions."

• Avoid using apologies that put you in a one-down position as a way of ensuring you're liked. Always begin from a place of equality—regardless of the level of person with whom you are dealing. He or she might have a higher position than you, but that doesn't make the person any *better* than you.

ACTION ITEM

Mistake 61

Using Minimizing Words

$\mathcal{A}$lthough women may not have cornered the market on the use of minimizing words, we certainly use them more than most men. Minimizing words are those that diminish the importance or size of an achievement. My cousin's seventeen-year-old daughter recently did it, and it served as a reminder that this is something learned early in girlhood in response to the message, *Don't brag or boast.*

During a family event, her grandfather proudly announced that she had won several scholastic awards. When I expressed my congratulations and inquired as to which ones, she responded, "Oh, they're *just* Golden State awards." Now, I have no idea what these awards are, but I do know she had to do something above and beyond the norm to achieve them. By using the word *just*, she minimized the importance of the recognition.

The workplace equivalent is to downplay success or attribute it to something other than talent, hard work, or know-how. In response to congratulations or compliments, women will often say something like, "It was really nothing," or "I guess I just got lucky." Say *those* phrases enough times and you'll begin to believe them.

COACHING TIPS

- Practice saying, "Thank you. I'm pleased with how it turned out." Say it over and over until it rolls off your tongue in response to a compliment.
- Objectively describe your achievements without using qualifiers. Avoid "It was only . . . ," "I just . . . ," or "I surprised myself . . ."
- If you want to be modest, try saying something like, "Thank you. I am quite proud of what I achieved and must give some credit to those who helped me along the way."
- Read *Power Talk: Using Language to Build Authority and Influence*, by Sarah Myers McGinty. This provides great insight into the importance of matching your communication to the situation as well as techniques for how you can ensure that your message is taken seriously.

ACTION ITEM

Mistake 62

Using Qualifiers

*A*nother way in which women calm their fears about being too direct, opinionated, or committed is to use qualifiers. They serve the purpose of softening, and weakening, your message. Qualifiers include comments such as:

"It's kind of like . . ."

"We sort of did . . ."

"Perhaps we should . . ."

"Maybe it would be better if . . ."

"We could . . ."

Yikes! It's maddening. Equivocating comments prompt people to ask or think:

"What *is* it like?"

"What *did* you do?"

"Should we or shouldn't we?"

"Is it better or isn't it?"

"Can we or can't we?"

COACHING TIPS

- Give your opinion in clear, certain terms. This doesn't mean dogmatically, just directly and without qualifiers.
- Here again, if you feel you need them, taglines can help you soften a strong opinion without invalidating it. For example, "I feel strongly that we should act now rather than wait for all the reasons mentioned. I'm curious to hear what others think."
- If you're really not sure, then preface your remarks with why you're not or what would make you more committed. "Given the facts we have so far, I'm not sure we should move so quickly. I would need more data before making a final decision," is still more clear than equivocating.
- Read Deborah Tannen's book *Talking from 9 to 5: Women and Men in the Workplace*. Tannen is the leading authority on workplace communication, and this book will help you understand the dynamics behind why some people are heard or viewed as authorities and others aren't. She makes no judgment about a superior or inferior style of communication, but rather seeks to have men and women better understand each other.

ACTION ITEM

Mistake 63

Not Answering the Question

$\mathcal{N}$ot answering the question can include an element of equivocating, but more often goes beyond it. Consider this exchange between a senior vice president and one of her direct reports:

SVP: Do you think we should tell our shareholders about the anticipated loss for the fourth quarter or wait until we're sure how much the loss will be?

DR: Well, we could tell them now in preparation for the fourth-quarter financials. On the other hand, if we wait we'll sound more credible in terms of actual numbers. If we tell them now we'll have to deal with lots of questions we can't answer. If we wait it may appear we're trying to hide something. There are pros and cons either way.

Guess what? The VP already knows there are pros and cons. She can probably articulate them just as well as you. What she wants is an answer. My Indonesian clients (who, regardless of gender, communicate in a stereotypically feminine way) call this *basa-basi*— "wishy-washy." Women often make the mistake of thinking they have the luxury of thinking out loud in response to tough questions. They believe putting all the options on the table is the most helpful and fair thing to do. The obvious problem is that it leaves the questioner without an answer. If you ask me, it's just another way women hedge their bets and play it safe. One colleague calls this "hiding in plain sight." If there ever is a time to make a declarative statement, it's in response to a direct question.

COACHING TIPS

- Directly answer the question you're asked. Just as in school, there are only four kinds of questions: true–false, fill in the blank, either–or, and essay. The question above was either–or; *Should we share the information now or wait?* The first words out of your mouth must be one or the other—or your own third alternative. In this case the sentence could begin with, "Neither. I think we should let the results speak for themselves when the financials are announced."

- The inability to answer a question directly and succinctly can stem from the desire to have the perfect or "right" answer. I often hear people answer a yes–no question with, "But I can't give you a yes–no answer." Oh yes you can. You do it by taking a risk and putting yourself on the line. It's better to err on the side of starting a debate than it is to sound wishy-washy.

- Use bottom-line thinking to organize your thoughts. Tom Henschel, president of Essential Communications, coaches clients to "chunk" answers mentally in terms of the bottom line and two or three pieces of supporting data. An appropriate response to the question above using this model would sound like this: "I suggest we share the information now. There are two primary reasons I advise this. First, I believe it's better to err on the side of full disclosure rather than be accused of withholding information. Second, we're pretty sure there's going to be a loss, but if we're wrong and there isn't, people will be relieved and we've lost nothing."

- When answering an essay question, use a numbered framework to order and express your thoughts: "I have three ideas . . . ," or "There are two paths we can take. . . ."

- Take an improvisation class. Part of being able to answer questions directly is knowing how to think on your feet. The techniques you learn in improvisation will be helpful to you in a number of ways.

ACTION ITEM

Mistake 64

Talking Too Fast

*W*omen, especially, suffer from this unique form of overcarbonation (see Mistake 76 for more discussion). Many of us, having been given the message that we talk too much, are fearful of taking up too much floor time. We speed up our communications so that we can get our entire message out before being interrupted or given a sign that we've talked too much. We wind up sounding like the man in the old FedEx commercial who could talk at the speed of light. Much like physical space, taking the appropriate amount of time to verbally express ourselves is a sign of entitlement. That is: *I'm entitled to be seen* and *heard.*

Because so much of your credibility is dependent on how you sound, regardless of the actual content, it's important to convey confidence, accuracy, and depth of thought. Speaking too quickly does just the opposite. It can be interpreted by others as implying that you don't deserve the time you're taking from them or that your message isn't important enough for them to spend time on. Rushing through your message can be construed as not being thorough or thoughtful in your approach. These interpretations can, in turn, cause the listener to question the accuracy of what you are reporting.

COACHING TIPS

- Practice speaking at a moderate pace. Practicing a presentation to music is helpful—provided it's not a Souza march.
- Join Toastmasters. These groups, which you can find in most cities, enable professionals to meet during the lunch hour and practice public speaking. Members give one another feedback at the end of each presentation. It's one of the best ways to gain comfort with not only talking, but public speaking, too. You'll find contact information in the Appendix.
- Ask a friend or colleague to discreetly give you a sign when your speech speeds up.
- Tell yourself you're entitled to take all the time you need to convey your message (providing you do it in the way suggested in previous tips).

ACTION ITEM

Mistake 65

The Inability to Speak the Language of Your Business

*E*very business and profession has a language and jargon all its own. We may joke about phrases such as *Stay on his radar screen*, *Push the envelope*, and *Paradigm shift*, but when we fail to use the language, it conveys a lack of familiarity. Influence comes from knowing the business, and one of the best ways you can exercise your influence is to use language unique to your industry and profession. Women often assume if they know and are good at their *piece* of the business, that alone will make them influential. Wrong.

One woman we worked with wondered why she was continually overlooked for promotions. She received consistently good performance reviews and was frequently praised for her expertise and contributions to the department. In an attempt to identify high-potential employees, her company regularly administered management assessments to a certain level of staff. The assessment included a few tests and an interview with an organizational psychologist. The results: She was described in the report as being of above-average intelligence, a good problem solver, and potentially a good manager, but lacking in her ability to speak about parts of the business other than her own.

Do you know the ROI, bottom-line, and performance indicators for your company? If not, it's time to find out.

COACHING TIPS

- Read the *Wall Street Journal*. It will provide you with not only information that could be helpful to you in your work, but also a common language of business.
- Ask someone in your finance department to explain the basics.
- Subscribe to industry magazines or newsletters.
- Take a class in accounting for nonfinancial professionals.
- Get involved with your own personal finances and budgeting.
- Attend professional association meetings.
- Research benchmarks and best practices in your field.

ACTION ITEM

Mistake 66

Using Nonwords

Nonwords are habitual sounds and phrases you use to fill up silence. When they infuse your speech, they make you sound unsure or hesitant. Nonwords can be *uh* or *er*, but can also be actual words like *Know what I mean* or *See*. Any repetitive sound used as a substitute for a brief pause becomes a nonword and detracts from your message.

If every sound you utter were transcribed, uh, well, you wouldn't, uh, want your speech to read as if you, uh, didn't know what you were talking about, know what I mean? Becoming conscious of these credibility busters can be the toughest part of changing the habit. Once you begin to track your nonwords, no matter how diligent you are, you're probably hearing only about a tenth of the ones you actually say.

COACHING TIPS

- Ask a trusted colleague for feedback about your use of non-words.
- Set up a real-time feedback loop with friends or colleagues. For example, over a cup of coffee have them snap their fingers every time you use a nonword.
- Involve people outside work in your real-time feedback. The more feedback you get, the faster you'll break the habit.
- Videotape yourself making a presentation and review it for how you sound.
- Put an audiocassette recorder on your desk and hit the RECORD button before you answer or dial the phone. Listen to the tape later and count your nonwords.
- Become comfortable with silence—it can be a powerful tool in your communications.

ACTION ITEM

Mistake 67

Using Touchy-Feely Language

*Y*et another way women display their insecurity around being direct is to use the proverbial touchy-feely language. The best way I can describe this to you is to show you what it sounds like in comparison to non-touchy-feely language (I feel wishy-washy just writing it!).

Touchy-Feely	More Confidently Stated
"It feels like we should . . ."	"I believe it would be best to . . ."
"I might . . ."	"I intend to . . ."
"You could consider . . ."	"I would advise you to . . ."
"How would you feel if we . . ."	"What would you think if we . . ."
"One could argue that . . ."	"The opposition would say . . ."
"My thought is that we . . ."	"My proposal is that we . . ."

You get the picture. Both sides convey the same literal messages, but the ones on the right side are more assertive. They make a stronger statement about the speaker's commitment to what's being said and about her desire to become visible. You might think I'm just splitting hairs here, but our language strongly conveys meta-messages about us, our values, and our intentions.

COACHING TIPS

- Practice beginning your sentences with declarative *I* statements such as *I think, I believe, I propose, I intend, I would like,* or even, *I feel.*
- Take more risks around stating your thoughts with conviction.
- Develop a more businesslike vocabulary by reading books and articles targeted to businesspeople.
- When writing letters or e-mails, go back and edit them with the intention of strengthening your written word.
- Don't entirely relinquish touchy-feely language—just be more discriminating in how you use it. It can serve a purpose when counseling or coaching coworkers.

ACTION ITEM

Mistake 68

The Sandwich

I don't know who came up with the idea for giving feedback using the sandwich technique, but it's manipulative and undermines your ability to be straightforward. The sandwich model suggests that when you're giving feedback you should couch the negative between two pieces of positive feedback. Fageddaboudit. It doesn't work. It may be easier for *you*, but not for the recipient. I hesitate to give you an example of how it works because I don't want you to get the idea you should include it in your communication skills repertoire, but for the sake of clarity, here's what it would sound like:

> Greg, I'd like to talk to give you some feedback about your recent work on the Jackson project. I really like how you spent considerable time up front building a relationship with the client. They seemed to appreciate it. On the other hand, I would have liked you to put more time into doing the research necessary to create a robust proposal to them. Overall, I'd say you're doing a good job of managing the client's expectations.

Now, what is Greg going to walk away with? He's going to be asking himself if he's doing a good job or not. Even though the last message was a positive one, the middle, more critical message, is most likely what he's going to focus on. Separating positive and negative feedback is a much more effective way of delivering a clear message of expectations and reinforcing appropriate performance. Giving critical feedback is difficult no matter how skilled or practiced you are at it. It's one reason why I use the seven-to-one rule of feedback (see the tips on page 174).

Women in particular often don't like being the bearers of bad news. In fact, most of us avoid it like a ten-pound box of chocolates. To be effective, feedback has to be specific, behavioral, and focus on positive results. A better way to approach Greg would have been as follows:

Greg, I'd like to give you a little feedback about the Jackson proposal. It seemed to me that the research you presented wasn't thorough enough and left a number of questions unanswered for the client [specific]. In the future, I'd like you to conduct a more thorough review of what the competition is doing and contrast the benefits of using our process and people [behavioral]. This would enable the client to make an informed decision in a shorter period of time [positive results].

COACHING TIPS

- Giving critical feedback is much easier if you've followed the seven-to-one rule. Over time you must give seven pieces of positive feedback for every one piece of negative. This enables the recipient to hear your developmental message and not see you as overly critical.
- When you give positive feedback, make certain it's free from *implied criticism*. Like a left-handed compliment, it sounds something like this from your mother-in-law: "Dinner tonight was just delicious. It's soooooooo much better than the last three meals you cooked for us."
- Keep in mind that ongoing feedback should be both positive and negative.
- Giving direct feedback can be made easier by using a model called the DESCript:

D = **Describe** why you're having the conversation.

Frank, I'd like to talk to you about something that happened last week when we were together on the Acme project.

E = **Explain** in behavioral terms how you see the situation and **Elicit** from the other person his or her perceptions.

I felt the bulk of the work fell on my shoulders because you arrived late and left early four of the five days. I'm wondering how you see the situation.

S = **Show** that you've heard what's been said and **Specify** what you want to see happen.

I understand you had a family problem to deal with and if I knew that in advance I could have made different arrangements or asked that someone else work with me. In the future it would be helpful

if you would let me know when you're not able to devote 100 per-
cent attention to a project we're working on together.

C = Tie the desired behavior to **Consequences** (positive or
    negative, depending on the severity of the problem or
    length of time it's been discussed).

Thanks for hearing me out. If we find ways to communicate better
internally we can provide increased value to our clients.

Mistake 69

Speaking Softly

*W*hen I was about fourteen years old, I worked in a dry-cleaning store owned by a woman who was prone to migraine headaches. If you've ever been in a dry cleaner midday during the week you know there's a hum of machinery and pressing equipment. I was speaking quite loudly to someone working a few feet away and the owner came over and whispered in my ear, "Don't you know that young ladies don't speak loudly?" For many years after that I was careful not to speak too loudly for fear of sounding unladylike. Three decades later I realized the woman most likely had a headache and just wished I would keep quiet. I wonder how many other young women have been given the same message—and for perhaps the same reason.

The volume of our voices is one more way in which we can manage others' impressions of us. Women tend to have softer voices to begin with. When we speak softly, the message conveyed is one of uncertainty or lack of confidence. Volume also impacts body language. The louder you speak, the more gestures you tend to naturally use. By combining appropriate volume and gestures, you immediately convey a sense of authority or subject-matter expertise.

COACHING TIPS

- When speaking before a group, pretend the person farthest away from you is a little hard of hearing, and speak loudly enough so that he or she can hear you.
- Take a voice, acting, or singing class to learn how to project your voice.
- If people tend to ask you to repeat things or to speak more loudly, consider this message something you must address.
- Videotape yourself either making a presentation or even just discussing a subject in a meeting. If you find it difficult to hear what you're saying, but everyone else can be heard just fine, this is another indicator that volume is something you want to work on.
- Listen to your own voice-mail greeting. Objectively assess how you would characterize the voice on the other end. Practice leaving a message that expresses self-confidence—this is frequently other people's first impression of you.
- Imagine your listeners as customers. Your voice should envelop them so they lean back comfortably in their chairs. If they have to lean forward, straining to hear you, you're not taking good care of those customers.

ACTION ITEM

Mistake 70

Speaking at a Higher-than-Natural Pitch

*W*hy is it that a woman can be speaking with another woman in a natural pitch—but when a man comes into the room, she's suddenly a falsetto? This is not something you usually catch a man doing. When a woman's voice reverts to sounding high and thin, it becomes like a little girl's voice. What does a little girl's voice sound like? Coy, demure, sweet, and not at all authoritative. Which is probably the effect some women *want* their voices to have.

Again, people respond not only to the content of your message, but the sound of it as well. Higher-pitched messages, which are stereotypically more feminine, tend to be discounted. Why do you think for so many years during early broadcasting that newscasters were all men? Walter Cronkite was someone we trusted even though we knew little about the man's character. To this day, male voices predominate in the national evening news. From Tom Brokaw to Peter Jennings and Dan Rather, men are the so-called voices of authority.

Although I can't tell you why it happens, I do know that lower voices are accorded more attention and respect. As voices go up in pitch, credibility goes down. Perhaps it's simply ingrained in our culture that lower voices are typically male, and we tend to grant more authority in general to men. Even men who have higher-pitched voices face the same problems with credibility as do women. Ross Perot's somewhat diminutive physical stature, combined with a voice that was higher-pitched than normal for most men, didn't help him in the political arena.

Think about the voices of Margaret Thatcher and Queen Elizabeth. Although the queen is largely seen as a titular head of state and Thatcher was elected to office, the differences in the pitches of their voices contribute to how seriously we consider one over the other.

COACHING TIPS

• When you wake up, make a noise. It can be any noise, like *Ummmmmmm* or *La la la la la*. You'll notice that this is your natural, unconstricted pitch—one you should try to maintain throughout the workday.

• Join a choral group and find your pitch. You won't be able to sing falsetto for long.

• Consciously breathe and relax your neck and shoulder muscles. Vocal pitch often rises because of tension and the restriction of the vocal cords.

• Imagine your neck and chest cavity to be large, spacious openings. Picture your voice rolling around inside you. Reframe any small, constricted images of your voice.

ACTION ITEM

Mistake 71

Trailing Voice Mails

$\mathcal{W\!e}$ used to joke that my mother-in-law didn't know how to say good-bye. Long after she and I had finished discussing the last item on either of our agendas, she just couldn't bring herself to close the conversation. The same holds true for many women when they leave voice-mail messages. Regardless of how succinct and articulate the initial part of the message is, it winds up something like this: "Okay, well, I guess that's everything. Uh, call me if you have any questions. That's it, I think. Okay. 'Bye." Trailing voice mails can undo the effectiveness of your initial (and most important) message. They can make you look indecisive.

I once worked with a client who told me that people left her rude, abrupt voice mails and that she didn't know how to respond to them. I asked her to save a few for me to listen to during one of our meetings. I also asked her to save some of her own voice-mail messages by asking trusted colleagues to forward them back to her. Upon listening to both sets of messages, it was immediately evident that those she had problems with were from men. They weren't rude and abrupt; they were just succinct. Hers, on the other hand, used more words than necessary as she thought out loud and scrolled through her mental agenda. In comparison, they sounded softer—because they *were* softer. More words soften a message. Fewer words make it more memorable.

COACHING TIPS

- Most business voice-mail systems give you the opportunity to go back and listen to your message. To find out if you're guilty of leaving messages that trail off, go back and listen to a few before sending them.
- In advance of your call, create a mental checklist of what you want to cover so you'll know when you're finished and it's time to hang up (my mother-in-law could have really used this tip).
- If you find that this is a mistake you make, force yourself to end after you've made your point. Stop talking. Say good-bye. Hang up.
- Prepare a standard tagline for the end of messages (voice mail or otherwise). Saying something like "Call me if you have questions," and hanging up immediately will work.

ACTION ITEM

Mistake 72

Failing to Pause or Reflect Before Responding

I'm sure you've heard the term *pregnant pause*. It's a brief period of time that causes others to anticipate and pay attention to what you're about to say. In your desire to please others and not take up too much time, you may respond to questions too soon, not giving yourself enough time to reflect on your answer. A pregnant pause before speaking is a powerful tool to add to your communication skill set. Remember the old commercials: "When E. F. Hutton talks, people listen."

A pause before speaking does several things. It conveys a message of thoughtfulness about what you're about to say. It generates interest on the part of the listener. A pause and the ensuing silence give others the impression you're self-confident. And they give you time to put your thoughts into a concise framework.

COACHING TIPS

- Practice counting to three before replying to a question—even when the answer is on the tip of your tongue.
- During the pause, ask yourself what the main point is that you want the listener to take away. Let that point be your lead sentence.
- Use the second hand of a clock or watch to time a three-second pause. In the middle of a conversation it may seem to you like an eternity, but as you will see, it's only momentary.

ACTION ITEM

Chapter 7

How You Look

When I coach, I typically begin with behaviors that are easily identifiable—and changeable. It gives people a quick success, because others can readily observe the efforts they put into replacing self-defeating behaviors with more functional ones. This section examines the things you may unconsciously or habitually do that contribute to perceptions of being less capable and competent than you really are. Don't be fooled by the apparent simplicity of some of these mistakes. Few women make only one of them, and when you combine several, it *significantly* contributes to the appearance of diminished competence.

Let's start by dispelling the biggest myth of career mobility: *The best and the brightest are rewarded with promotions and choice assignments.* Wrong. Those who possess a competitive degree of competence *and* look and sound the part of a professional are the ones who move fluidly through their careers. Competence is only table stakes. It's what gets you in the door. It's expected that you'll be competent, but competence alone won't move you forward.

Research shows that about 55 percent of your credibility comes from how you look. How you sound accounts for an additional 38 percent. Only *7 percent* of your credibility is based on what you say. If you don't look the part, you won't be recognized as a competent professional—no matter how smart or educated you are. Fortunately, it's also one of the easiest things you can address on your path toward forging the impression that you are a credible and competent professional.

Mistake 73

Smiling Inappropriately

We reached the point in a Leadership Skills for Women workshop where we were discussing how to get people to take us more seriously. A petite Asian woman, an engineer from the Jet Propulsion Laboratory in Pasadena, California, raised her hand to question why her male colleagues ignored her input. When she finished, a ripple of laughter crossed the room. The reason was obvious to the rest of us: *The entire time she spoke she displayed a rather large (and inappropriate) smile.*

Girls are socialized to smile more than boys. Parents smile more at girl babies than at boy babies. When men don't smile, they're taken seriously. When women don't smile, we're often asked, "What's wrong?" It's no wonder we aren't even aware when we smile at the wrong times.

COACHING TIPS

- Pay more attention to when you're smiling. I constantly coach women to "watch the smile."
- Consciously match your facial expression to your message. You don't want to put a stamp on with a steamroller, but you do want there to be congruence between your body language and your message.
- Before delivering serious messages, rehearse in front of a mirror. This will give you a better idea of when you're smiling inappropriately.
- Don't quit smiling entirely—it contributes to your likability quotient, and likability is a critical factor in achieving success.
- Be discriminating about how and when you choose to smile. For example, it can be intentionally used to soften a less serious message or to convey empathy.

ACTION ITEM

Mistake 74

Taking Up Too Little Space

The use of space is one way we make a statement about our confidence and sense of entitlement. The more space you take up, the more confident you appear. The next time you're on an airplane, take a look at the differences between how men and women sit. Whereas men sit down and spread out using both armrests, women tend to keep their elbows tucked in close to their sides, trying not to take up too much space. Another place to observe this is on elevators. Most people, men and women alike, are conscious of making room for others as they enter. As the elevator gets crowded, however, it's more likely you'll see a woman cower in a corner for fear of taking up too much space.

The same phenomenon often happens when a woman steps in front of a room to make a presentation. She tends to stand in one place, moving only slightly within the space she occupies. When you combine taking up too little space with using too few gestures, the overwhelming impression conveyed is that of being demure, careful, unwilling to take risks, timid, or frightened with little to contribute.

COACHING TIPS

- When giving a presentation, use the full amount of space available to you by slowly walking side to side, forward and back. Even if you're on a large stage, you should come out from behind the podium to take up about 75 percent of the space available.

- Choose a seat at a meeting that will give you freedom to move around. Don't sit where you'll be forced to keep your elbows glued to your sides. Keeping your elbows on the table and leaning in slightly conveys a message of being more alert to what's being said.

- When standing in front of a group, stand with your feet about as far apart as your shoulders are wide.

- When seated, use the coaching tips on gestures provided under Mistake 75 to appear more expansive and less constrained.

- Request a lavaliere or handheld microphone when one is needed. It will allow you to move about more freely than if you have to speak into a stationary microphone.

ACTION ITEM ☐

Mistake 75

Using Gestures Inconsistent with Your Message

$\mathcal{T}$he use of gestures is an outgrowth of not taking up enough space. Like all other parts of your self-presentation, gestures should be integrated with your energy. If you're working to make your presence larger and to take up more space, working on your gesturing is an easy way to begin. The problem is, most women have never learned the art of gesturing. It's little wonder why. We've been taught to sit demurely with our hands folded in our laps. When we have used gestures, we've been given the message that we're too emotional. For fear of being called unladylike or emotional we've let the pendulum swing the other way—*no* gestures.

Comedian Joan Rivers is an example of someone who takes up lots of space with her gestures because she *wants* to convey the message of being larger than life. Her hair, makeup, and gestures all contribute to this impression. Unless you do stand-up comedy, I wouldn't recommend that you emulate her.

Senator Hillary Rodham Clinton, on the other hand, uses the prototypical gestures of a politician. She appears tense and almost *too* conscious of the use of gestures and often reverts to being an "ax gesturer." You know the move. It's when points are emphasized using repetitive karate-chop-like gestures. Predictable, consistent gestures distract from the message.

Gestures should complement, not detract from, your message. A woman who does this well is Elizabeth Dole. Her communications, including her gestures, convey the message of authority while simultaneously maintaining her elegance and natural femininity. The next time you see her on television, turn off the sound and just watch her. You'll see that she nonverbally communicates a sense of confidence without the brashness of Joan Rivers or the rehearsed look of Senator Clinton.

COACHING TIPS

- Allow your gestures to flow naturally from your spoken message and your energy.
- Be aware of when you wring your hands because you're anxious—and stop.
- Match your gestures to the size of your audience. The larger the group, the larger the gesture.
- Emphasize your points by enumerating them with your fingers (one, two, three).
- Communication consultant Tom Henschel advises clients to use gestures that "break the silhouette." That is, when you stand with your hands at your sides or in front of you, your silhouette shows no gestures. When you work on taking up more space, your gestures should move outside the line of that silhouette. You can do this whether you're sitting at a conference table or standing in a doorway having a chat.
- Put energy into your gestures and enjoy taking up the space!

ACTION ITEM

Mistake 76

Being Over- or Underanimated

$\mathcal{A}$ communication colleague—Allen Weiner, president of Communications Development Associates in Woodland Hills, California—uses the term *carbonation* to refer to a person's degree of animation. It includes not only gestures, but also facial expressions, speed of talking, and other forms of body language. We've all listened to and watched people who are *over*carbonated. They look and sound as if they were a can of soda that was shaken before being opened. Not only is it distracting, but it makes the person appear less confident than he or she may actually be. My contention is that women, more than men, are guilty of overcarbonation because they feel responsible for making everyone happy. As a result, they go out of bounds by putting more verbal and nonverbal energy into everything they do.

Conversely, if a woman has previously been given the message that she's too bubbly or emotional, she can fall into the trap of appearing *under*carbonated, or flat and unanimated. In an effort to conceal her natural ebullience, she causes the pendulum to swing the other way. We ascribe characteristics such as *low-energy, aloof, boring* (or *bored*), or *depressed* to such people.

The friendship between actresses Carol Burnett and Julie Andrews often puts them on the same stage, where we observe Burnett's overcarbonation as a counterpoint to Andrews's undercarbonation. Especially early in Burnett's career, her exaggerated facial expressions and body movements contributed to her success as a popular comedian. In comparison, Andrews is less animated, more cautious, and ever the demure lady. Neither set of behaviors conveys the message most professional women want to project.

COACHING TIPS

- If you tend to be undercarbonated, speak more loudly. It's a natural way of increasing your animation.
- Because overcarbonation can result from anxiety, practice deep breathing and other relaxation techniques that will reduce overly animated behavior.
- Consciously strive to strike a balance between over- and undercarbonation. One way to do this is to observe yourself on a videotape with the sound off. If you were standing outside the meeting, looking through a glass partition, how would you describe the woman you see?

ACTION ITEM

Mistake 77

Tilting Your Head

$\mathcal{T}$he tilt of a head in conversation has the impact of softening a message. It's almost always used to either imply a question, signal that you're listening, or encourage the other person to respond. Women tilt their heads significantly more than men in conversation, and in this regard a head tilt can be a good thing. When trying to convey a direct message, however, it can be interpreted as uncertainty or a lack of commitment to what you're saying—even when you're dead sure of it. It's another one of those ways women have learned to communicate difficult messages in a socially acceptable, but less assertive, way.

The best place to observe this is on television where people are interviewed. On Sunday-morning programs such as *Face the Nation, This Week,* or *Meet the Press,* you don't see too many head tilts—by either the host or the guest. The topics are often of national and international importance, and therefore participants in these discussions typically want to convey a sense of seriousness.

But if you watch skilled interviewers such as Jane Pauley, Barbara Walters, Stone Phillips, Phil Donahue, or Connie Chung conduct an interview in which they really want a guest to open up, they effectively use tilting of their heads. They can ask the most personal questions and get away with it because, in part, the tilt of the head makes guests feel as if the host is really interested in what they're saying.

So the message here is not to stop tilting your head entirely. But do be aware of when you might do it at difficult moments as a means of softening a message that *shouldn't* be softened.

COACHING TIPS

- When conveying a serious message, avoid tilting your head. Look at the person straight on and in the eye.
- Use a head tilt to your advantage—such as when you're listening and want the other person to open up or when you want to convey you understand how the other person may feel.
- A head tilt can also be used to bridge an uncomfortable silence—as if to say, *Take your time. I'm listening.*

ACTION ITEM

Mistake 78

Wearing Inappropriate Makeup

*M*akeup is tricky. On the one hand, I don't want to perpetuate Madison Avenue's image of what a woman *should* look like. On the other, I know it's something people notice when it's too heavy or too light. I once asked the boss of a woman scientist for feedback about what she could do to overcome existing barriers to promotion. He thoughtfully explained how she could be more strategic, speak up more in meetings, and be a stronger advocate for her staff. After an uncomfortable silence, I suggested it seemed like he had something to add. Somewhat sheepishly he said, "Maybe she could start wearing makeup." You can hear that comment as just another sexist remark—or as a valuable insight into what people expect as you climb the corporate ladder.

I was once shopping in Palm Springs, California, when I noticed a woman who was heavily madeup. Turning to a friend, I nodded and commented, "She looks like a caricature of Tammy Faye Bakker." As we approached the checkout line and I saw her husband at the time, Jim Bakker, join her, I realized it *was* Tammy Faye Bakker. In business you don't want to use Ms. Bakker as your makeup role model. Makeup is an accessory similar to a piece of jewelry or a scarf. People do notice it. Wearing too little can diminish your credibility as much as wearing too much.

COACHING TIPS

- Go to the makeup counter of a high-end department store and ask a salesperson (whom you consider to be appropriately madeup) for a free consultation.
- Ask a trusted colleague or friend who wears makeup that complements her features if she would be willing to give you feedback on yours.
- If you tend not to wear makeup, begin by using small amounts as recommended by a friend or consultant.
- Go to a Mary Kay or Avon consultant for helpful makeup hints.
- Stand with your back to a mirror and quickly turn around and look at your face. What's the first thing you notice? That may well be the place to use less—or more—makeup.

ACTION ITEM

Mistake 79

Wearing the Wrong Hairstyle

*H*air. Can't live with it. Can't live without it. Who hasn't struggled with a bad cut, not quite the right color, or just a bad hair day? The most common mistake I see women make is to wear their hair too long. One of the consultants in our office tells the story of when she received her doctorate in organization development and asked a physician in senior management at the hospital where she worked for feedback about how she could get a promotion she wanted. Looking at her beautiful waist-length strawberry-blond hair, he replied, "Lose the Alice in Wonderland look."

I may not like how he gave her the feedback but, as they say, feedback is a gift. In a predominantly male environment, long hair diminished her credibility by emphasizing her femininity. We'll never know if she got that promotion because she cut her hair— but even she agrees that cutting it made a difference in how people treated her.

COACHING TIPS

- Don't scrimp when it comes to finding a good hairdresser. A low-price leader may not be the best place to find a highly skilled professional.
- There's an inverse proportion of hair to age. Typically, your hair should get increasingly shorter as you get older and go higher on the corporate ladder. Not only is shorter hair more professional, but longer hair tends to emphasize facial features of which we may be less proud as we age.

- If you don't want to cut your hair, wear it up to give it the appearance of being shorter.
- Hair, like makeup, is an accessory. Make certain it complements the rest of your appearance.
- If your hair is graying, consider a good colorist. Whereas gray or graying hair on men is viewed as distinguished, women aren't typically afforded the same compliment.
- Mary Mitchell, in an article titled *Dress for Success: 9 Tips for Professional-Looking Hair*, offers these two tips:

1. Skip the Pat Benatar look. Heavily sprayed, crunched, and gelled hair can be "the equivalent of wearing a skirt slit up to the thigh," says Jennie Brooks, stylist for Ovations Salon in Philadelphia. Instead, she suggests products that provide a softer, more polished look that won't distract from your professionalism. "It's possible to have an edge while still being professional. Think of an altogether polished look."
2. Match your style to the vibe of your workplace, no matter what level you're at. At the prestigious Hotel Bel-Air in L.A., *all* employees are required to look sophisticated and yet low-key (so they fit in but don't rival guests like Meg Ryan, Sir Anthony Hopkins, and Nancy Reagan). The director of human resources, Antoinette Lara, tells employees, "Think about how you'd wear your hair at a club on a Saturday night. Then do the opposite when you come to work."

ACTION ITEM

Mistake 80

Dressing Inappropriately

*T*he workplace casual trend has made professional attire a bit more complicated. It used to be simple. Women wore dresses or suits to work. As casual dress, including slacks and pantsuits, becomes increasingly acceptable, the margin for error increases. Follow the maxim, *Dress for the job you want, not the job you have,* and you won't go wrong. Short skirts, seductive clothing, stiletto heels, unshined shoes, and ill-fitting or wrinkled clothes won't get you where you want to be—at least not in the business world. Like it or not, people notice not only the *style* of clothes we wear, but also their *quality*.

Are there exceptions to the rule? Absolutely. There's a brokerage firm I work with that has a fairly strict and conservative unspoken dress code. When I coach women from this organization and the issue of dress comes up, as a way of arguing the point they inevitably bring up one woman who breaks every single rule of dress outlined above. I mean *every* rule. And to this I reply, "She's the exception and not many of us get away with being exceptions." It just so happens the woman is superb at what she does, has been with the company for many years, and is known for being eccentric. Not only her dress, but also her behavior is tolerated because of the value she adds. Most of us wouldn't get away with it—and shouldn't even try.

COACHING TIPS

- Look around at the successful women in senior positions in your organization. *That's* how you should dress.
- Even if your office subscribes to workplace casual, dress just a little better than most of the people around you.
- When you know you're going to be making a presentation, dress up. You'll rarely go wrong wearing a dress or suit.
- Go to the department that sells professional women's clothing at Nordstrom, Bloomingdale's, or other similar stores and ask for fashion advice.
- View clothes purchases as an investment in your future. Budget enough money to buy several really good outfits a year. When you feel good in clothes, you act more confidently.
- Have your color chart done. Wearing colors that complement your natural features has a bigger impact than you might think.

ACTION ITEM

Mistake 81

Sitting on Your Foot

I'm not sure I would have thought of this one myself. It comes from Dr. Doug Andrews, chair of the School of Business at the University of Southern California. He has the opportunity to observe students, both young and older than average, in his classes. He described it as "this thing women do when sitting where they tuck one foot up underneath them." Dr. Andrews is absolutely right when he says it's something that he never sees men do and that it conveys the impression of being a little girl rather than a professional woman. I was recently in an antiques store where I was drawn to a photograph from the early 1900s of a six- or seven-year-old girl posed for her portrait. She had one foot tucked under her, and it softened both her and the picture.

You can also observe this phenomenon on television talk shows. A guest comes out, sits in the chair next to the host, and tucks her foot up beneath her. Can you imagine Bill Gates, George W. Bush, Mel Gibson, or Samuel L. Jackson doing this? It's almost always a woman guest who does it, and she does it out of discomfort or shyness. It may be cute, but it's not professional.

COACHING TIPS

- It's simple. If you want to be taken seriously, sit with both feet on the floor with knees together. In a more relaxed situation, cross your legs at the knee. *Never* sit with your foot tucked beneath you.
- Remember, being "grounded" requires "both feet on the ground."

ACTION ITEM

Mistake 82

Grooming in Public

*W*hen was the last time you saw a man pull out a mirror and check his hair after lunch? How about file his nails during a meeting? Even the thought of it is ridiculous. No matter how discreet you think you're being, grooming in public is noticed and mentally logged by those around you.

Another habit (often unconscious) that women often reveal is that of flipping long hair behind the ears. It may be when she looks down to read something or it may be used as a coy, flirtatious gesture. Take a moment to think about a group of people who "play with" their hair. If you came up with teenagers, you're right. Flipping your hair behind your ears makes you appear less mature than you really are. Public primping emphasizes your femininity and detracts from your credibility. Real women avoid PDG (public displays of grooming).

COACHING TIPS

- Never comb your hair or apply lipstick in public. If you can't resist, excuse yourself and go to the ladies' room.
- If you do go to the ladies' room to primp, keep it quick. Don't keep people waiting at the table. Better yet, wait until you get back to the office.
- If you see your reflection in a mirror or glassy surface and notice something wrong, avoid the inclination to fix it there. Wait until you can do so in private.
- Avoid touching your hair unnecessarily. Think in terms of, *Every time I touch my hair I reduce my credibility by one year.*

ACTION ITEM

Mistake 83

Sitting in Meetings with Your Hands under the Table

*S*itting in meetings is not the same as sitting at the dinner table. You don't have to follow the rules learned in childhood for keeping your elbows off the table. Observe how men sit at meetings. When they're speaking, confident men almost always lean in with their elbows and hands resting on the table. When men begin listening to something that intrigues them, you can picture them sitting with their elbows on the table, chin resting on their clasped hands.

And what do *we* do? We often do as we were taught—sit coyly with our hands folded in our laps or under the table. The difference is striking. As uncomfortable as it may be at first, when it comes to being taken seriously, all research points to the need to "put it on the table."

COACHING TIPS

- In meetings, lean forward slightly, resting your forearms on the table with hands lightly clasped. Not only does it make you look more involved in the conversation, but it also puts you in a perfect position to gesture when needed.

- While we're on the subject of meetings, let me slip in two more tips. Whenever possible, select a seat next to the most powerful person in the room. For some unknown reason, that person's power permeates those around him or her. It also conveys the message that you're not afraid of power.

- Don't be afraid to sit at the head of a long or oval table. Again, this isn't the Thanksgiving dinner table. From the head of the table, you can see everyone in the room and, just as important, everyone can see you.

ACTION ITEM ☐

Mistake 84

Wearing Your Reading Glasses around Your Neck

$\mathcal{T}$his habit surely had to start with some librarian in the 1950s. Why is it that women, not men, buy those little chains to hang reading glasses around their necks? Are we more apt to lose our glasses than men, or are we just more willing to call attention to the fact we're aging? In some department stores you'll even find these chains displayed as accessories.

Similarly, at a workshop on developing presentation skills there was one woman, apparently in her mid-fifties, who held on to her glasses throughout her videotaped half-hour practice session. Not only did she hold on to them, but she also twirled them while listening to questions from the audience. Never once did she actually put them on—leading me to believe they were more a prop than a requirement.

At the risk of sounding ageist, I need to say once again that, unlike men, it's the rare woman who finds her credibility increasing with age. Although I don't think it's something to hide or lie about, I do think it's not necessary to emphasize it.

COACHING TIPS

- If you're concerned about being able to read your notes during a presentation, type them in a font large enough to see without glasses. Using a PowerPoint presentation will also serve to keep you on target with your topic without having to put your glasses on and take them off.

- If you need a prop, use a marker or a pencil. There's nothing wrong with holding it; just take care not to tap, twirl, or click it, thereby creating a distraction from your message.

- A trick my ophthalmologist taught me is to wear a pair of plain glasses with the readers on the bottom. Even though I wear contact lenses to camouflage my severe nearsightedness, I wear the glasses over them so that I'm not continually putting on and taking off my readers.

- Since we're on the subject of glasses, keep in mind they can be used as a prop to make you appear more mature if you have difficulty with being taken seriously because you look too young. Even if you don't require corrected vision, a pair with nonprescription glass can give you the appearance of being a bit more mature.

ACTION ITEM

Mistake 85

Accessorizing Too Much

*A*ccessories can be your best friend—or your worst enemy. I recently watched a videoconference in which former secretary of state Madeleine Albright was a keynote speaker. She wore a lovely tailored dress—totally appropriate for the event—but she had on her trademark huge pin. To me, this detracted from her message: Throughout the presentation I found myself focusing more on trying to figure out what the pin was than on what she was saying.

I've learned to use accessories to manage the impression I often give that I'm very serious. In an effort to convey an impression of more levity, I accessorize with playful pins. One that frequently gets attention is of three women with wild hair and colorful dresses, arm-in-arm. It's my way of getting across the message: *I may be serious, but I like to have fun as much as the next person.* Of course if I'd been given feedback that I was too jocular, my tactic would be different.

Carefully chosen, accessories add style and personality to other-wise conservative corporate attire. They convey a message about you that may not be heard through your words and presence alone. But when inappropriate or overdone, they detract from your credi-bility. Accessories make a statement. Consider what you want yours to be.

COACHING TIPS

- Don't wear long, dangling earrings to work. Depending on your size and hair length, aim for posts—no larger than the size of a quarter.
- Add an inexpensive pearl necklace and earrings to your accessory kit. They never go out of style.
- Match accessories to not only your outfit, but also what you will be doing that day. A whimsical pin might be appropriate for a day in the office when you're meeting only with colleagues, but not necessarily for one when you're making a strategic planning presentation.
- Similarly, the bigger the group you're speaking to, the bolder the accessories can be. Just be certain not to make the same mistake as Secretary Albright.
- Do the same as was suggested in the section on makeup tips. Turn your back to the mirror and quickly swing around. Does anything stand out about your accessories? If so, consider changing it.

ACTION ITEM

Mistake 86

Failing to Maintain Eye Contact

$\mathcal{T}$here are a number of factors that contribute to the tendency to avoid another person's eyes. In some cultures it's a sign of respect to look away when speaking with someone who is older or has more authority or stature than you. There's research that suggests avoiding eye contact is a sign of deception. Children won't look at us when they know they've done something wrong or when they're being scolded.

When a woman avoids eye contact, it's usually a sure sign she's uncomfortable or unsure of herself. If the eyes are the window to the soul, then you must use them to allow others to see your sincerity, self-confidence, and knowledge, and to see the other person's. A good place to observe this behavior is on television when someone like Connie Chung, Jane Pauley, or Barbara Walters conducts an interview. Each of these women has learned the art of eye contact. Note how they look people directly in the eye, especially when asking difficult questions. Similarly, note that when they're embarrassed or someone has said something that catches them off guard, they look away. What also makes these women so good at what they do is that by looking the other person in the eye, they often get a sense of what he or she is thinking and base the next question on this. You don't have to be a television interviewer to use eye contact to your advantage.

COACHING TIPS

- When you go to the movies, observe how the more self-confident female characters use their eyes to convey a message. Make a mental note of the specific behaviors that contribute to this impression.
- If you have been given the feedback that you have a tendency to stare, get into the habit of looking slightly up or to the side when thinking about a response. This creates a break in the eye contact long enough to convey a comfortable pause.
- When greeting someone, be certain to look him or her in the eye. It puts you on an even footing with the person.

ACTION ITEM

Chapter 8

How You Respond

So far we've looked at the behaviors in which you actively engage that detract from or diminish your credibility. In this last section we'll examine how you respond to the ways others treat you.

Many women have been socialized to respond to inappropriate treatment in a polite, docile, or acquiescent way. One tragic example of this is a woman who told me what happened to her at a movie when she was about seven or eight years old. She and her older cousins routinely went to a Saturday matinee. One Saturday a man sat down next to her and began to molest her. She allowed this to continue for several minutes then told her cousins she wanted to change seats, but not why. When they moved, the man moved along with them and began doing it again. She became immobilized. She allowed it to happen until the movie was over.

In relating the story many years later she wondered why she hadn't told him to stop or asked her cousins for help. Sadly, her response isn't unusual for women. We're not taught to defend ourselves or get angry when someone is disrespectful to us. In my book *Women, Anger & Depression: Strategies for Self-Empowerment* (Health Communications), I contrast the messages little boys are given regarding anger to those given to little girls. Whereas boys are typically taught the art of self-defense, girls are taught to turn the other cheek. As a result, we're more likely to tolerate behavior we should never allow to happen. Unlearning those early childhood messages is a huge step on the path to living an empowered life.

Mistake 87

Internalizing Messages

*P*arents are guilty of giving children all kinds of messages that they carry with them for a lifetime. Not all of these are negative, but they do impact our self-esteem and how we see ourselves in the world. Whether it's "You're just like your father—you'll never amount to anything" or "You're such a sweet girl. You're going to grow up and get married and have lots of children," the message sets the stage for a self-fulfilling prophecy.

The messages are also not always verbal. Sometimes they're implicit expectations for how you should behave. Much of my coaching work begins with helping clients get in touch with those early-childhood messages and examine the impact they have on the present. Our greatest strengths are often learned in response to implicit and explicit parental expectations or demands. As a result, we tend to over-rely on these and are reluctant to relinquish ones that are no longer effective.

Let me give you an example. Claudia was the oldest of seven children in her family. Both parents were alcoholic and depended on her to help raise the younger kids. As with many children who come from alcoholic homes, she was hypervigilant, very responsible, and quite protective of her siblings. No one *told* her she had to do this; she just did. These same behaviors served Claudia well early in her career. Her supervisors appreciated how she would show initiative, take new team members under her wing and show them the ropes, and always be on top of potential problems or barriers to achieving departmental goals.

Later in her career, however, these *identical* behaviors kept her from reaching her full potential. What was once viewed as being on top of problems was now described as being too critical. Whereas her willingness to take new people under her wing was once appreciated, now she was seen as intrusive and overly controlling. And one of her greatest strengths, initiative, was now interpreted as "grandstanding"—trying to get the best projects for herself.

Claudia had internalized the messages of childhood all too well—even though they were never actually verbalized. This will give you an idea of how well we must internalize *verbal* messages. Our work with Claudia was not to get her to stop doing all those things that served her well early in her career, but rather to provide her with a set of alternative behaviors from which she could choose when the situation called for it. For example, rather than always volunteering for difficult assignments, she needed to be more conscious of who else might benefit by learning from this project. And rather than being quick to point out mistakes, she might let some of the smaller ones go so that others could learn from them and not view her as quite so nitpicky.

COACHING TIPS

- Ask yourself which lesson learned in childhood contributes to your greatest strength and what complementary behaviors may be required to balance the strength.
- Read Alice Miller's book *The Drama of the Gifted Child* (also available on audiotape). This book illuminates how some adults respond in inappropriate ways as the result of parenting that either placed unrealistically high expectations on them or instilled a sense of worthlessness (and at times those are interrelated). It's helpful in that it provides a framework that allows you to act more consciously rather than through internalized messages.
- There's a tape that plays in our heads with childhood messages. When the messages on that tape hold you back from achieving your goals, use self-talk to tape over it. Consider therapy if the messages are so strong that you have difficulty taping over them.
- Post in a conspicuous place and frequently recite Eleanor Roosevelt's famous maxim: *No one can make you feel inferior without your consent.*

ACTION ITEM

Mistake 88

Believing Others Know More than You

$\mathcal{B}$etty is an organization development consultant with her own practice. For many years prior to forming her consultancy, she was an organization development manager at the corporate headquarters of a nationally known fast-food chain. Between the two experiences, she can legitimately be called an expert in her field. One day she met with a prospective client who wanted to talk to her about doing a team-building session. As this aggressive, know-it-all executive laid out the problem, Betty began to think it wasn't team building he needed, but a conflict resolution intervention between two employees.

After the executive finished explaining what he wanted and why he wanted it, Betty suggested that team building might not be the appropriate path to take. She pointed out that when there is conflict between two employees and you do a team-building program, you may not get the results you want and needlessly include other team members in their dispute. The executive wouldn't listen. He had used consultants in the past for situations such as these and he knew how they worked. He was certain the situation would be improved through the team building.

As with many consultants, Betty had to weigh the client's wishes against her best professional judgment. Does she walk away from the business opportunity to prove her point, or could she possibly help this group using the methodology demanded by the client? In the end she opted for the latter and facilitated a two-day off-site for the executive's department of twelve staff members. She thought that perhaps he was right—he made a convincing case for the off-site and Betty was open to giving it a try.

The team building proved to be a total disaster. The majority of the time was spent trying to mediate the conflict between the two individuals whom the executive had mentioned in their first meeting. While at first Betty used the interaction between these two as a learning opportunity for everyone present (teaching listening and negotiation skills, for example), eventually the team tired of the tension in the room and began to mentally check out. In the end the conflict was never resolved, and the other team members felt that the experience was a waste of their time.

Betty learned the hard way that women often underestimate how much they know and put more stock in a stranger's opinion than in their own wisdom. From doctors to car salesmen, we think others know better. Betty acquiesced to the executive's assertion that he knew better than she—and the results were catastrophic. Her reputation within the company was damaged, and the executive wound up blaming her lack of expertise rather than recognize she was correct in her initial diagnosis and recommendation. In the long run she would have been better off saying no to the opportunity. Unlike men, we tend to admit it when we don't know something—but fail to trust ourselves when we do. Men can tell us something entirely wrong with more authority than any woman ever will. Worse yet, we believe it.

COACHING TIPS

• Before assuming someone knows more than you, ask a few probing questions to determine his or her expertise. "Why do you recommend that?" or "How do you know that?" will at least convey the message you're not a pushover.

• Before asking someone else's opinion, be certain you really need it. As discussed earlier, asking a question to which you know the answer can diminish your stature.

• If something doesn't sound or feel quite right to you, it probably isn't. Buy time to think by insisting on a time-out to consider what's been suggested.

ACTION ITEM

Mistake 89

Taking Notes, Getting Coffee, and Making Copies

*A*t any minute during any given day there has to be a woman somewhere in the world tearing her hair out about this problem. How many times have I heard a man say, "Let's have _____ [fill in the blank with any woman's name] take notes. She has the best handwriting." Or, "Linda, would you mind making the coffee?"—as if it's really a question.

In workshops and seminars women frequently ask, *What should I do when I'm asked to make coffee for or take notes at a meeting?* The easy answer is, *Don't do it.* What's harder is avoiding it. Each time we accept one of these tasks, we perpetuate the stereotype that a professional woman's role is to nurture, care for, and serve others at work. The inevitable result is that we either feel badly about ourselves or angry at the situation. Neither solves the problem. How can you respond to inappropriate requests? Well, it just so happens I have a few coaching tips.

COACHING TIPS

- Tell your boss about how you feel being given these tasks and suggest that the responsibilities be rotated. If he or she tells you it's no big deal, respond simply and nondefensively with, "It's a big deal to me."
- When asked in front of a group if you'll make copies or take notes, practice saying in a neutral, unemotional way, "I think I'll pass since I did it last time."
- Show you're a good "meeting manager"—make a checklist of meeting tasks and suggest that the department administrative assistant be assigned them.
- Introduce your corporate culture to the custom of having the newest person on the team perform these tasks.

ACTION ITEM

Mistake 90

Tolerating Inappropriate Behavior

*D*ebra was transferred to a developmental assignment in the finance department at her company headquarters in December. She was given an office on the executive floor—but when she arrived, she realized it had no desktop computer. *Simple*, she thought. *I'll just call the IT group and get one.* When she called, she was told there was none currently available but there should be one she could have in about a week. Two weeks passed and no computer. She called once again, and the IT manager apologized. His wife just had a baby and her request slipped between the cracks. The computer intended for her had been given to someone else (a man, of course). He'd see what he could do. By now it was Christmas and her office was closed for two weeks.

I met with Debra in her office in mid-February—still no computer. She showed me a note she'd written to the IT manager:

> I understand you've been quite busy and that you are short-staffed. However, I think two and a half months is a bit long to wait for a computer I need to perform my work. I would appreciate it if you would get the computer to me as soon as possible.

What's wrong with it, you ask? It's too understanding, too understated, and not specific. Here's my edited version:

> It's been two and a half months since I first asked you for a PC and, despite numerous promises, I still have not received it. Since this seriously impedes my ability to perform my job, I will expect one in my office no later than Friday. If this is not pos-

sible, or it does not arrive, I will assume it is due to matters out of your control and ask your boss and mine for assistance. Please call later today to discuss further.

This **Describes** the problem. **Explains** why it's a problem. **Specifies** desired outcomes. Lays out **Consequences.** It contains all the elements of the DESCript described under Mistake 68.

COACHING TIPS

- Take a self-defense class. Defending yourself physically will shift your thinking about defending yourself verbally.
- Use more *I* messages as opposed to *You* messages. The latter tend to be more confrontational and point the finger rather than solve the problem. Listen to the difference. Turn this:

You're always interrupting me!

Into this:

I would appreciate it if you would let me complete my sentence.

Or turn this:

You can't do that to me!

Into this:

I'm not happy with how I've been treated. I'd like to offer some alternatives.

- Don't swallow your feelings—they'll only catch up with you in one way or another. Get in the habit of asking yourself how you *feel* when you're treated less than respectfully and express it in the form of an *I* message.

"I feel like a child when I'm spoken to in that way."
"I feel disrespected when my ideas are ignored."
"I feel I'm being taken advantage of."
"I feel I'm entitled to a reason why my request is being denied."

• Just because you don't react in the moment doesn't mean you don't have the right to go back and revisit an inappropriate encounter. When you're taken off guard, it can be difficult to come up with the right words. It's your prerogative to go back later and say, "I was thinking about something that happened yesterday and I'd like to tell you how I felt about it."

• Read *Since Strangling Isn't an Option: Dealing with Difficult People, Common Problems, and Uncommon Solutions,* by Sandra Crowe. It will help you see the ways in which you might unknowingly contribute to interpersonal conflicts and methods for defusing them.

ACTION ITEM

Mistake 91

Exhibiting Too Much Patience

*I*t may be true that all good things come to those who wait, but women take the maxim to an extreme. When the term *impatient* is applied to a man, it means he's a go-getter, always on go, or ready to move ahead. When the same term is applied to a woman, it means she expects too much, has a sense of entitlement, or doesn't understand how it works around here. Patience is *not* a woman's virtue.

In Kyoko's case, she was told to just be patient and she would get a promotion she had been promised. So she waited. And she waited. And she waited some more. After six months of waiting, her boss was transferred to another division. When she asked him about the promotion before he left, he told her the new person would handle it. Of course you know what happened. The new person came in and knew nothing about the promotion—nor did he care. Granting promotions wasn't exactly high on his list of priorities.

COACHING TIPS

- The squeaky wheel does get the grease—and it won't soil your skirt. One executive told me he has no problem if someone pushes him once, pushes him twice, but three times is too many. Until you've pushed at least once, you haven't advocated for yourself.
- Don't believe it when someone tells you you're impatient. It's only a way to get you to quit bugging him or her.
- When you're told to be more patient, ask the person to give you an idea of when you should revisit the matter. If he or she suggests a time too far in the future, press for a time frame that meets your needs. "That's much longer than I had anticipated or we had originally discussed. Why don't we say in two weeks rather than a month."
- If you're asked to wait longer than you think is needed, ask, "Why so long?" There may be a legitimate reason; if there isn't, you can explore other options you may have.

ACTION ITEM

Mistake 92

Accepting Dead-End Assignments

*T*here comes a time in everyone's career—man or woman—when an assignment is offered that has DEAD END written all over it. To take it or not to take it—that is the question. And the answer is: *It depends.* Don't be quick to accept an assignment just because you think you're supposed to or you don't want to appear ungrateful. You never know where it might lead. On the other hand, it may only lead to a dead end.

I once coached a young woman who was offered a transfer to a small, remote division of her company. Not only that, the division was losing money. Anxious to prove she was capable of turning around a struggling division, and wanting to make her mark so she could move on to bigger and better things, she took the job without a second thought. If she had only done a little more inquiring about the division and the person previously in the position, she would have found that he was leaving because there were rumors that the division was about to be sold. She'd been there only eight months when the deal was announced and she wound up working for a much smaller and less prestigious company. Don't think it didn't cross my mind that she was offered the transfer because she was (1) a woman, (2) young, and (3) naive.

COACHING TIPS

• Never accept *any* assignment before first checking it out. Find out what the company has planned for the particular department or division, how it is perceived by others in the company, why the position is vacant, and to what future jobs the position typically leads.

• It's better to err on the side of turning down a dead-end job than accepting one in which others have failed in or languished. You'll know this only if you do your homework in advance.

• Consider the following five factors a plus when deciding whether or not to take what appears to be a dead-end assignment:

1. It has accessibility to senior management.
2. There's potential for advancement within twelve to eighteen months.
3. You have unique skills that would turn the dead end into a freeway.
4. It allows you to significantly expand your network of contacts.
5. You have nothing to lose.

• Consider the price of taking a lateral assignment. Although these can often be good opportunities to acquire new skills, they also delay upward mobility. If the economic situation is such that there aren't many upward opportunities or the organization is flattening, a lateral is a good move. Otherwise, ask around about how men in similar situations have been treated and ask that you be treated the same.

ACTION ITEM

Mistake 93

Putting the Needs of Others Before Your Own

*A*s women, we frequently find ourselves in positions where our needs come second to those around us. Whether it's taking care of a disabled parent, delaying your education until your husband completes his, or canceling your plans because a child has asked you to do something for her, the results are the same. Your needs don't get met. Of course, there are times when this can't be helped or it's the only right thing to do. But when it becomes the norm rather than the exception to the rule, it's time to take a look at what you do to perpetuate it.

In the workplace we see the phenomenon manifest itself when there are limited funds, perks, or opportunities. Wanting to play fair or be kind, a woman will put her requests on hold or lower her expectations. Pretty soon she feels as if she has no choice at all and doesn't see that *she* has created the problem.

COACHING TIPS

- Make sure you know what you need or want by routinely asking yourself what it is. Many times women are so accustomed to denying their own needs that they no longer know what they are.
- Between work and home, stop for twenty minutes and do something for yourself. It can be dropping by the library to read the newspaper, going to a park and listening to music, or calling a friend from your cell phone.
- Learn to negotiate. Whether you read a book or take a class, it's important that you are familiar with the many techniques of negotiation. For example, did you know it's been proven that those who *ask* for more wind up *getting* more? Or that by dividing up your needs like a salami and asking for just one piece at a time, you are more likely to have all your requests approved?
- Avoid giving in just because it's easier or you don't want to make waves. This is another place where reading the book *The Shadow Negotiation: How Women Can Master the Hidden Agendas That Determine Bargaining Success* (mentioned earlier) would be helpful. The authors of this book go beyond just providing techniques; they also help illuminate the self-sabotaging ways women often enter into negotiations.
- As many times as it takes to believe it, tell yourself it's not selfish to have your needs met—even though it might inconvenience others.
- Make sure you have a life outside work that you want to go home to. Workaholism is often an excuse for not having a life.

ACTION ITEM

Mistake 94

Denying Your Power

*W*hen I had a private psychotherapy practice, I intentionally chose downtown Los Angeles for the location of my office. I wanted to serve the large community of businesswomen who spent the better parts of their lives working in corporations around the city. My clients were well-educated and successful women. They also had something else in common: They could not see or acknowledge their own power.

As these women told me stories of how they were taken advantage of, ignored, or in other ways abused at work, I would often say something like, "How is it that a powerful woman like yourself allows others to treat her that way?" To a person, the response was to deny she was powerful. "Powerful? I'm not powerful," was a typical reply. And this became the focus of my first book, *Women, Anger & Depression: Strategies for Self-Empowerment.*

When I examined the phenomenon more closely, it became apparent that women denied their power because of the messages they received growing up. Power was associated with men and, as such, was a masculine term. Their perceptions of power had to do with who was in control—and they knew *they* weren't. Just looking at the top of most major corporations still proves this. As of this writing only eleven women are at the helm of the nation's one thousand largest companies.

Juanita is an example of someone who, in denying her personal power, found herself depressed and falling short of her career aspirations. She was an attorney with one of Los Angeles's most prestigious law firms. She had been with the firm almost five years and didn't seem to be getting anywhere. Younger, less experienced male lawyers who joined the firm after her were given higher-profile client cases and, in some situations, more paralegal assistance. Needless to say, this contributed to feelings of depression and incompetence. Eventually, it became a catch-22 for Juanita—as she struggled with her depression, she was given even fewer "meaty" cases, which in turn exacerbated the depression.

As we explored why these other lawyers seemed to be surpassing her professionally, Juanita expressed resignation over the fact that it was simply an "old boys' club" and there was little she could do to change the situation. In other words, she felt powerless. When I suggested that she had more power in the situation than she was giving herself credit for (even if it was only to pick up and leave), she denied she was in any way powerful.

It's not an insignificant fact that Juanita came from a family where she was the only girl among six children. Her father, a Mexican immigrant, presided over a traditional household where the boys were revered and Juanita was pretty much viewed as "just a girl." And so my work with Juanita was about helping her find and define her own brand of power. Without that, I knew the depression would continue and she had no chance of either improving her work situation or finding a job where she would be better respected.

As is the case with so many women, Juanita had to redefine *power*. She knew her father and brothers were powerful—and she wasn't anything like them, ergo she must not be powerful. We talked extensively about different kinds of power and that for women it isn't about controlling others, but about having control of one's own life. Denying your unique brand of power erodes self-confidence and perpetuates a self-fulfilling prophecy. It was only after many months of taking baby steps in expressing her needs with both her family and her boss that Juanita's depression gradually lifted and she was able to see the connection between power and having responsibility for her life's direction.

COACHING TIPS

- Read my book *Women, Anger & Depression: Strategies for Self-Empowerment*. (How's that for branding and marketing?) It's designed to be a workbook to help you first identify childhood messages about power and anger and then find ways to express yourself in more empowered ways.

- Redefine *power* by considering the ways in which you have more control than you allow yourself to use. For example, you have the choice to say "enough" when you're being exploited or to say "no" to unreasonable requests. In many ways *this* book is about reclaiming your power.

- Use self-talk or posted affirmations to reprogram how you think about power. For example, write, "I am as powerful as I choose to be" or "Only I determine how powerful I am," and post it near your desk where only you can see it or in a portfolio you take to meetings.

- When someone suggests you're powerful, accept the compliment gracefully—even if you don't feel it at the moment. Over time the belief will become part of your self-messages.

ACTION ITEM

Mistake 95

Allowing Yourself to Be the Scapegoat

*E*va is a human resource representative with a well-known toy manufacturer. She was providing counsel to an employee who was struggling with her relationship with a very difficult boss. One day Eva got a call from her own boss, the division's vice president of human resources, who told her that the woman's boss (also a vice president) wanted to fire the woman. Eva suggested she call the boss and schedule a meeting with him and the employee for the purpose of facilitating a dialogue. Wanting to preserve his own power in this scenario, the HR vice president said no; he'd arrange it. Eva, understanding the politics involved in such situations, agreed to let him broker the meeting.

When she heard nothing about the meeting, Eva called the HR vice president and left a message asking if the meeting had been arranged. She heard nothing back. She sent an e-mail. No reply. Based on feedback she was getting from others, it seemed things were improving, and Eva assumed the meeting wasn't necessary. Then she got a call from the woman's boss. He wanted to meet immediately. When Eva showed up for the meeting, the HR vice president was there, and the woman's boss was apoplectic over the fact Eva hadn't made an appointment to come talk to him. The HR vice president, who'd insisted on scheduling the meeting himself, sat there silently. Eva could say nothing to assuage the man's anger as he ranted for the next forty minutes about *her* (Eva's) ineptitude.

Talk about sticky situations. If Eva told the man that the HR vice president had said he would schedule the meeting, she risked losing the support of her boss. If she didn't, she was the scapegoat. She decided it was better to be the scapegoat than to risk having two vice presidents angry with her.

COACHING TIPS

- Diplomatically let people know you don't like being scape-goated. What Eva should have done was speak with her boss after the meeting and let him know he failed to support her. Without pointing a finger or blaming, she could have said something like, "I'm confused over what just happened in there. It was my understanding that *you* wanted to schedule the meeting. I left several messages for you and never heard back." At this point her boss would have only two choices. The high road would be to admit his mistake and apologize. Not likely to happen given the fact he'd sat silently in the meeting and let her take the heat. More realistically, he'd tell her it was *her* responsibility to follow up. Either way, just having the conversation would let him know she didn't appreciate being scapegoated, and would be her best shot at preventing it from happening again. Is this to say it wouldn't happen again? No—only that she'd put him on notice that she recognized what just happened and was unwilling to silently shoulder the blame.
- Other language you can use to avoid being scapegoated:

> "There's no need to point a finger or assign blame, but I want you to know I followed the instructions I was given. Why don't we focus on how to move forward?"
> "I'm happy to redo the report if it's not what you want, but I would like to make clear it was prepared in accordance with our policy related to confidential information."
> "What would be helpful to me in the future would be if we all would meet together to review the process. It seems different departments had different ideas about what the end product would look like."

ACTION ITEM

Mistake 96

Accepting the Fait Accompli

*Y*our office is redesigning its work spaces. There are two large offices with windows and three smaller interior ones available for staff of your department at your same level. When the floor plan comes out, you notice you've been put in one of the smaller offices while a male peer who has been with the company less time has been given one of the larger spaces with a window. When you speak with the space planning department about it, you're told, "Too late. The plan has already been submitted to office services and they'll be setting up the phones and computers next week."

If you accept what they say, you've accepted the fait accompli—a French term meaning "an irreversible or predetermined decision." It's a technique people use when they don't want to change their plans. When it comes to dealing with women, they often bet on the fact you won't argue and will accept it as fact. It's also used as a negotiation strategy. An insurance company will send you a check to settle a claim before they've even spoken with you. They're betting you'll cash it rather than go to the trouble of contesting the amount.

Women are far more likely than men to go for the bait. Whether it's accepting a lower performance rating than you expected or a less convenient time to take vacation because you've been told, "That's just how it is," you've taken less than you're entitled to without an argument. If you're like most women, you'll find a way to rationalize the decision and wind up believing it's what you really deserve. Instead, use the tips on the following page to enhance your negotiation skills.

COACHING TIPS

- If it's important to you, don't accept less than you deserve without a fight. There are times when it won't be worth winning the battle only to lose the war, but there will be others when the principle matters.
- Always accompany your complaint with a proposed solution. Using the scenario of the offices on the previous page, an example would be, "Then it's not too late. The phones haven't been moved yet. I suggest the offices be assigned based on seniority or some other objective factor."
- Use the "broken record" to counter claims of fait accompli. Like a record with a scratch, you repeat your concerns, using different words, as many times as necessary to engage a dialogue. Here's how it works:

SPACE
PLANNING: Too late. The plan has already been submitted to office services and they'll be setting up the phones and computers next week.

YOU: Then it's not too late. The phones haven't been moved yet. I suggest the offices be assigned based on seniority or some other objective factor.

SPACE
PLANNING: I've already sent all the plans and change requests to office services.

YOU: It may be inconvenient, but they haven't taken action yet. I'm sure adjustments could still be made based on a more equitable method of assigning space.

SPACE
PLANNING: I really don't have time to redo the forms.

YOU: I would be happy to help you once we agree on a fair way to assign space.

SPACE

PLANNING: I don't have the authority to make the changes.

YOU: Who does? I will speak with them or we can meet together.

The broken record doesn't always yield the desired results, but it sure gives you a good shot at it—especially if you do it without anger or judgment.

ACTION ITEM

Mistake 97

Permitting Others' Mistakes to Inconvenience You

*T*his story, a variation on the scapegoating and time-wasting themes, demonstrates how one woman handled being inconvenienced by her boss's mistake. Maria was an internal efficiency expert who went from division to division of a defense company, providing expert advice on streamlining processes. Before she went to one particular location, her boss told her that what the plant wanted was simply an outline for a training program. She developed the outline and met with the plant manager, who expressed disappointment over the brevity of what she had to offer. What he expected was a full curriculum with accompanying materials and for her to facilitate the training program. Maria appropriately told the manager it was her understanding all he wanted was an outline, but she would double-check with her manager.

When she called her manager, he told her to just go ahead and give them what they wanted. She was dumbfounded. Maria, being an efficiency expert, had scheduled her work around other plant requests and didn't have the time to prepare a project of this magnitude. When her boss reiterated the need to give the plant manager what he'd asked for, she realized she was going to be working long nights and weekends for the next several weeks. His failure to ask the right questions of the plant manager caused her to be greatly inconvenienced.

Maria was savvy enough to know she had to do it, but wanted to be sure this didn't happen again. Although she could have talked to the boss about it directly, she felt that this was too confrontational for her. Instead, the next time he gave her an assignment, she said, "Let me be clear on what the expectations are here—I don't want to be in the situation again where I show up unprepared as happened last month." She then repeated her understanding of the requirements and added, "If, when I get there, it turns out to be more complex and require more time than I'm allotting, will I have your support in letting the plant manager know we'll have to reschedule his project?" Perfect! She tactfully let her boss know she didn't like what happened last time and wasn't going to be held responsible for his failure to get the facts straight at the outset. Although she can't control what the boss does in the future, she can make every effort to preclude its happening again.

COACHING TIPS

- Assess the risk against the profit of meeting unreasonable expectations caused by someone else's mistake. There will be times, as in Maria's case, where you'll have no choice but to put in the time needed to meet a customer's needs. But there will also be times when you have the latitude to push back by saying something like, "This wasn't what we originally discussed and agreed to. Since I'll have to rethink the plan and put more time into it than I anticipated, I won't be able to have it completed within the initially proposed time frame."

- Before rearranging your life to correct someone else's mistake, try to negotiate a win–win solution. Let the person know you want to provide the best service possible—and that to do so, you may need more time or resources. Ask for what you realistically need to do the job in a reasonable manner.

ACTION ITEM

Mistake 98

Being the Last to Speak

*O*h, boy. This one is a big problem for women. I've conducted workshops and team-building programs for women as well as mixed groups for more than twenty years. There's a particular exercise I do that involves giving the group a problem and ambiguous instructions for solving it, then observing how participants respond. In all that time, with literally thousands of participants, I can count on one hand the number of times a woman was the first to speak in the exercise when there were both men and women present.

The inclination to hold back when men are present is a huge mistake. Whether it's a small team meeting or a larger group, those who speak early and often are seen as more credible, greater risk takers, and possessing more leadership potential than those who speak later. Speaking early in meetings shouldn't be confused with being pushy or domineering. Nor should you worry about being accused of talking just to hear your own voice—I'll give you some tips that will make that unlikely. The longer you wait to speak, the more likely it is that someone else will say what you're thinking—and get credit for it.

COACHING TIPS

- In a group, be among the first two or three people to speak, and speak every ten to fifteen minutes thereafter.
- If you can't be among the first to speak, make sure you're not the last.
- You don't always have to give an opinion when you speak. Supporting what someone else has said, asking a legitimate question, or commenting on an emerging theme are equally good ways to make your presence known without appearing as if you like the sound of your own voice.

ACTION ITEM

Mistake 99

Playing the Gender Card

*P*art of my career was spent as an equal employment specialist. In this position my responsibilities included investigating and responding to scores of claims from sex discrimination to violations of the Rehabilitation Act. The common thread through 90 percent of these cases was not discrimination, but poor management. And like it or not, poor management is not illegal. Despite the fact there are also laws to protect those who file claims of discrimination from retaliation, I never saw a claim that helped *anyone's* career. It didn't always hurt, but it never helped.

There is no doubt in my mind sex discrimination is a real part of a woman's employment experience. Except in egregious cases where the discrimination is so blatant it cannot be defended, a company will make every effort to protect its reputation, its management, and its staff. I distinctly remember investigating one case in Texas where a woman said she was discriminated against by her boss because she was a woman. Her claim was that he verbally abused, demeaned, and embarrassed her in front of her peers. Interviews with nearly twenty employees revealed he didn't do this just to her—he did it to *everyone*. Using this as the defense, the company won the case. When it was over, the manager received no more than a slap on the wrist.

In another case, a woman filed an internal complaint that she was treated differently than her male colleagues when it came to assignments. Despite the fact that my investigation showed she was right—she *was* treated differently and for no apparent reason other than that she was a woman—the company opted to defend the manager's decisions. She filed a claim with the Equal Employment Opportunity Commission, but before it could be investigated she was terminated for what I thought was fabricated "cause." It took the commission nearly a year to investigate her claim, find in her favor, and order her to be reinstated with full pay and benefits retroactive to the date of termination. She did come back to work but, as you might imagine, it was so uncomfortable that she eventually quit voluntarily. She may have won the battle, but she lost the war.

Even if you don't go so far as to file a formal internal or external charge of sex discrimination, there is a stigma attached to women who "make noise" publicly about it—people suddenly become uncomfortable with you. They begin to act differently around you and treat you more carefully. In most cases this is counter to what women want—to be treated fairly. These are a few reasons why I strongly urge women to explore every other alternative available to them before playing the gender card.

COACHING TIPS

- Before suggesting there has been sex discrimination, try directly confronting the problem from an objective standpoint. Identify the manifestations of the problem, not the causes. For example, if you think you've been overlooked for a promotion because you're a woman—don't go there at first. Instead, ask your boss or human resource representative why you didn't get the job and what you should do to be considered a better candidate in the future.

- Don't try to change the system alone. You'll wind up being a martyr. If enough other women feel as you do, then form a task force to look into the issues, define the problem objectively, and propose solutions.

- Think long and hard before verbalizing concerns about sex discrimination to anyone in your company. It's not something companies take lightly. Many have adopted stringent zero tolerance policies, which means any suggestion of discrimination will be immediately and thoroughly investigated. Once you put the ball in motion, it's often impossible to stop it.

- If gender is a legitimate impediment to success in your current workplace, you have only three options: Put up with it (which I don't recommend—it will only further diminish your self-esteem), pursue the formal internal channels for addressing it (which may or may not yield the desired results), or leave (which is the only option over which you truly have control).

ACTION ITEM

Mistake 100

Tolerating Sexual Harassment

$\mathcal{N}$o woman should ever feel she has to tolerate sexual harassment, which is different from sex discrimination. Whereas *sex discrimination* refers to decisions made on the basis of gender, *sexual harassment* refers to decisions made on based on a woman's willingness or unwillingness to respond to requests for sexual favors or tolerate an intimidating, hostile, or offensive work environment. There isn't *quite* the same stigma attached to a claim of sexual harassment, because most smart employers know women do not make the charge frequently or frivolously.

A general rule used by many labor lawyers is the "one bite of the apple" theory. A coworker gets one shot at asking you out on a date. Once you say no thanks, the person has had his (or her) one bite of the apple, and further propositions may be construed as sexual harassment. Since it's socially acceptable to date coworkers, one bite of the apple can be defensible. The situation is quite different, however, when the coworker is senior to you. Given the norms around workplace dating, it is incumbent upon you to make your wishes clearly known when you have no interest in the other person.

COACHING TIPS

- In the case of quid pro quo harassment (requests for sexual favors), your first and best recourse is to tell the harasser in no uncertain terms the behavior is not wanted or welcome. In the case of environmental harassment (making the workplace uncomfortable or intimidating), you should similarly let it be known that you want the jokes, innuendoes, or comments to stop. Once you say "No" or "Stop," it moves from socially acceptable behavior to harassment.

- If the behavior doesn't stop immediately, ask your human resource department for help. If you simply want it to stop and don't want to pursue it further than that, they'll most likely speak with the person and that will be the end of it. It's important that you not tolerate the behavior—allowing it to persist can give the impression you liked it at one time, then changed your mind.

- If, after speaking with human resources, the unwanted behavior continues or if there is retaliation of any kind, consider filing a formal internal charge of sexual harassment. At this point an investigation into your allegations will most likely be conducted. Outcomes can vary from a verbal warning to transfer or termination of the offender.

ACTION ITEM

Mistake 101

Crying

$\mathcal{Y}$ou *had* to know I would get here sooner or later. To rephrase a line from Tom Hanks in *A League of Their Own*, "There's no crying in baseball—or the office." You don't need a Ph.D. to know many women cry when they're happy, when they're sad, when they're frustrated, when they're angry, when the sun is shining, when it's not—well, you get the point. While most women know they shouldn't do this at work, there are just times when you can't help it. You don't need an example—you've either seen it or done it. Let's cut straight to how you can at least minimize it or recover professionally from it.

COACHING TIPS

- Don't substitute tears for anger. Women often cry because they've been taught being angry isn't ladylike or acceptable. When you feel the tears well up, silently ask the question, *What's making me angry?*
- When you do cry at work, immediately ask to be excused. Don't sit there bawling. It only makes people uncomfortable. By removing yourself temporarily from the situation, you let others off the hook (which they'll appreciate) and give yourself time to become composed. Make it a stock response to say, "I hear what you're saying. Give me some time to think about it and get back to you."
- Studio City–based psychotherapist and business coach Susan Picascia provides her clients with these four tips:

1. Put words to the tears and focus on the problem instead of your feelings. Say something like, "As you can see, I have strong feelings about this. Why don't we focus on specific outcomes to solve the problem?"
2. Don't be seduced by seemingly humanistic organizations (hospitals, nonprofits, and the like) into thinking crying is okay. Crying gives people the impression you're not in control, not competent, and weak. We like to think there is room for these very human, very real emotions in the workplace. But we're not there. People have negative associations with crying in the workplace—and it crosses gender lines. Women are no more compassionate than men in this arena.
3. If you find yourself welling up frequently or easily, you may want to look inside with a good friend, coach, or psychotherapist. We cry when we're on overload, angry, anxious, hurt, or for a reason appropriate to a situation. If you're welling up

a lot, you may find your thinking is too negative or catastrophic. Few things in the workplace are life and death or so dramatic they can't be addressed reasonably well. Keep your emotions from causing you to think the worst. Think positively about what may seem like a very scary experience and you will cry less.

4. When someone goes for your jugular in a personal way, don't go for the bait and do set him or her straight. Focus on the content of your conversation by saying something like, "Stan, this is not about me overreacting, this about a workload problem we need to solve."

ACTION ITEM

Appendix: Personal Development Planning and Resources

A goal without a plan is a dream, and a plan without a goal merely passes the time. Now that you've spent time reading this book, it's time to make a plan for how you will achieve your goals. This is where the rubber meets the road. You can say you're going to do things differently, but like the story of the pig and the chicken who were both asked to bring something to breakfast, *commitment* makes the difference.

Go back through each of the chapters and take a look at the action items you've checked. Before completing the development plan provided, look for commonalities and categorize the items into three to five behaviors you believe will make the most difference for you. Then go ahead and write down what you commit to doing differently as a result of having invested your time and money in this book. You'll find a sample line to use as a model to get you started.

Resist the urge to get carried away with too many commitments. You really can't work successfully on changing more than just a few things at a time. Besides, it's not the number of things you change that's important, but selecting those few behaviors that will make the biggest difference. I once had the opportunity to interview Wimbledon champ Julie Anthony, who now coaches several women players on the tennis pro tour. When I asked her about the secret of creating meaningful change, she told me if you focus on one thing, other change occurs naturally. For example, she would never tell a player to focus on changing her grip, her stance, and her forehand all at once. Anthony pointed out that by just changing the grip, the player will find her stance and forehand changing along with it.

The same holds true for you. You don't have to worry about being more concise, less apologetic, having a stronger handshake, and wearing the right clothes to work all at the same time. Do just one thing—and do that well—and you'll find over time there will be a subtle shift in many other behaviors. The point of coming up with three to five items for your personal development plan is so that as you master one, you can check it off and move on to the next.

You'll notice there's also a column for "resources." The remainder of this chapter provides you with books, courses, magazines, and other resources to help you develop the skills that will bring you closer to achieving your professional goals. You don't have to reinvent the wheel; just go through the list and select those that seem most appealing to you and realistic in terms of your actually utilizing them. Don't set yourself up to fail. This isn't a diet. Stretch yourself but don't make it so difficult that you'll want to abandon your plan after a week.

Finally, remember that growth is a process of two steps forward, one step back. This is what clients report to me all the time. In the beginning it seems as if you'll never quite get the hang of it. Before long, it's second nature—unconscious competence. As the Chinese philosopher Lao-tzu said, "A journey of a thousand miles must begin with a single step."

This is where I leave you. It's been a pleasure sharing my experiences and those of my clients and colleagues with you. I would be delighted to hear from you with your comments, success stories, and areas where you get stuck. I can be reached by e-mail at info@corporatecoachingintl.com. Every letter I get is answered (although it sometimes takes me a little while), so don't hesitate to write. You deserve to have your questions answered, and I would value your feedback.

CHART 5

PERSONAL DEVELOPMENT PLAN

ACTION ITEM	COMMITMENT	START DATE	RESOURCES
Speak more concisely	Ask for feedback from Roberta after each team meeting. Mentally plan what I'm going to say before speaking.	October 1	Read: *You Are the Message*

COACHING

Obviously, I'm a proponent of business coaching. I've seen first-hand how it helps good performers distinguish themselves as great performers in comparison to their peers. Prospective clients often asked for statistics related to the results of coaching. The data collected in my own firm indicates that about 60 percent of the people we coach are promoted within one year. An additional 10 percent choose to leave their current jobs and/or employers as a result of coaching and go on to more satisfying positions or companies that are a better match for them. Ten percent of those coached remain in their jobs doing better than before, but not enough so that they are considered high performers. And in about 10 percent of our clients we see no change at all due to their lack of commitment to the process or other intervening factors.

A variety of factors contribute to results. Is the client paying for the coaching or is the company? When it's the latter, there may be less sense of urgency about getting the most possible from the process. Is the client in a position that's well suited for him or her? If not, no amount of coaching will enable him or her to achieve maximum potential. What are the goals coming into the process? If the focus is on being promoted, the likelihood of promotion increases. If it's to get better at his or her current position, then that's what usually happens.

Another factor is the coach himself or herself. During the past decade, the field of coaching has exploded with interest on the part of practitioners. It's been only in the last three to five years that it's become an organized discipline with professional associations and standards. Many people are currently entering the field—and some are great coaches, while others haven't had the business experience needed to help clients understand the many nuances of business. Coaching, like any other field, consists of people with a wide variety of experience and expertise. My suggestion is that before investing money in any coach, you ask him or her these questions:

- How long have you been in practice?
- What did you do before you were a coach?
- Do you have any particular credentials or licenses to coach?
- Are you a member of any professional coaching associations?
- Before I decide to work with you, may I have the names and phone numbers of current or former clients whom I can call for a reference?
- What services are included in your fee?
- In what area do you consider yourself a coaching expert?
- Have you actually worked inside a corporation or have you been a consultant for your entire career?

The answers to these questions will give you an idea of whether you're dealing with a seasoned professional or someone new to the field with little business background. I personally find the business background critical—it's what I look for when hiring coaches. There are many psychologists moving into the field as personal coaches, but they lack the practical experience needed to understand workplace dynamics. They may be well qualified to help you address issues related to stress or relationship issues, but if they haven't experienced the realities of life inside a corporation, they may not be as qualified to assist you with the subtleties that contribute to success.

Because it's impossible for me to know all the reputable coaches currently in practice, I will provide you with a listing of only those with whom I am personally familiar. I've also included the Web site of a professional association that will enable you to locate other coaches in your area. As with any service—*caveat emptor.*

- **Corporate Coaching International**
  http://www.corporatecoachingintl.com
  877-452-2654
  What kind of coach would I be if I told you to market yourself, then left out my own coaching firm? In 1995, after two decades

working in the field of human resources both inside and outside corporations, a colleague and I developed the concept of team-based coaching. This unique approach allows each client the opportunity to work simultaneously or sequentially with several coaches, each with a particular expertise. Our focus is on leadership development, team building, and one-on-one coaching. You can learn more about our coaches, take a coaching quiz, and find complementary resources at our Web site.

- **International Coach Federation**
  http://www.coachfederation.org
  In addition to general information about the coaching process, the Web site of this professional association of coaches allows you to sort potential matches using a variety of factors including discipline, location, price, and more. Once you've logged on to their site, go to the Coach Referral Service link.

- **Christine Belz**
  Belz & Associates, Inc.
  55 Public Square, Suite 1715
  Cleveland, Ohio 44113
  216-664-1877
  Belz@ex100.com
  Christine Belz is a seasoned coach with experience working both inside corporations and as an external consultant. She takes a team approach to coaching: Not only the client, but also his or her boss and peers participate in a process in which developmental work is integrated into the business.

- **Christine Cowan-Gascoigne**
  The Leadership Company
  21308 Halburton Road

Beachwood, Ohio 44122
216-991-9517
christinecg@hqcom.com
Christine founded the Leadership Company in 1990 to foster responsible leadership. Her driving belief is that quality leadership, not quality strategy, determines organizational and individual success. She coaches in a wide variety of areas including influence skills, power sources and uses, visioning, and time management.

- **Agnes Mura**
  http://www.agnesmura.com
  Santa Monica, California
  310-450-5035
  Agnes is a Master Certified Coach, founding board member of the Professional Coaches and Mentors Association, and president of its Los Angeles chapter. She travels throughout the United States and Europe helping executives develop increased skill in strategic thinking, achieving bottom-line results, managing change, and building relationships.

- **Christine Reiter**
  Time Strategies
  P.O. Box 884
  Pasadena, California 91102
  626-795-1800
  chrisdr@pacbell.net

Time Strategies coaches clients who are constantly challenged by paper flow and time management. Solutions are customized to meet each client's needs to enable better management of paper, time, and technical resources. Out-of-the-box techniques are used for clients who are frustrated by traditional approaches to time and paper management.

WORKSHOPS AND TRAINING PROGRAMS

As with coaches, the quality of workshops and workshop leaders runs the gamut. If you've ever attended a training program, you're probably already on the mailing lists of many firms who provide public workshops. Other consulting firms conduct only private workshops for the employees of companies that pay their fee. Given the choice, I would advise you to take company-sponsored classes simply because the facilitator should be familiar with your company and its unique requirements for success. There are a few firms, however, that I recommend based on the outstanding programs they offer in specialized areas. You'll find these listed below.

Before signing up for any program, remember that the purpose of training is to increase your skill in a particular area. Here are a few suggestions to maximize participation in training programs:

- Set specific goals or skills you want to take away as a result of attending the program.
- Sit in the front of the room. This will cause you not only to pay closer attention, but also *get* more attention from the facilitator.
- Fully and actively participate. As a trainer, I know that those who participate the most, get the most out of the program.
- Don't be afraid to ask questions—especially ones that relate to you personally. Facilitators appreciate participants who seek practical ways to apply their classroom learning.
- Prepare a summary of the key themes to share at a future team meeting. If you know in advance you're going to do this, you'll

participate in a different way than if you're not expected to share the learning experience.

- After the program, thank your boss for the opportunity to attend and discuss with him or her what you learned. There's no better way to assure you'll be allowed to attend future programs.

- **NTL**
http://www.ntl.org
800-777-5227
I *highly* recommend NTL to clients who want to gain increased insight into their workplace behavior and how others perceive them. Founded in 1947, it is the premier provider of experiential programs. I encourage you to visit the NTL Web site and explore the spectrum of experiential programs it offers.

- **American Management Association**
http://www.amanet.org/seminars/index.htm
800-262-9699
AMA seminars are geared to every organizational level—from chief executive officers to administrative professionals, from senior executives to first-time managers. These small-group, team-learning experiences are dynamic and interactive. Seminar leaders are active business professionals with years of hands-on experience.

- **Dale Carnegie Training**
http://www.dalecarnegietraining.com
Although I've never attended a Dale Carnegie program myself, I'm told by people who have that they're professionally done and can really make a difference in how you see yourself and interact with others. In addition to workshops related to increasing confidence, public speaking, and widening your per-

sonal horizons, they offer classes that can be used toward continuing education credits (CEUs) and college credits.

- **Toastmasters International**
  http://www.toastmasters.org
  949-858-8255
  Toastmasters is not really a training program, but organized groups of businesspeople who meet weekly for the purpose of improving their skills in conducting meetings, giving impromptu speeches, and preparing more formal presentations. There are more than eighty-five hundred chapters in seventy countries around the globe—and if there's not one convenient for you, the Web site contains information about how you can start one. One woman I referred to Toastmasters told me it *significantly* increased her self-confidence and platform skills.

- **Outward Bound**
  http://www.outwardbound.com
  888-882-6863
  Learning by doing is the premise of Outward Bound courses. If you've never challenged yourself physically, you'll find it can be a powerful way to learn survival skills that will help you not only in the wilderness, but at work, too! You may captain a boat, lead an ascent, or navigate your group through difficult terrain. These opportunities allow you to realize the success of your own decisions and plans, as well as learn from your mistakes.

- **Business Media Training**
  http://www.seminarinformation.com
  888-337-2121
  This Web site contains a full listing of training programs that are provided not by this firm itself but other training firms. The

site thus appears to be unbiased in recommending the best training solution to meet your needs.

BOOKS AND AUDIOTAPES

9 Steps to Financial Freedom: Practical and Spiritual Steps so You Can Stop Worrying, Suze Orman (Three Rivers Press, 2000).

Be a Kickass Assistant: How to Get from a Grunt Job to a Great Career, Heather Beckel (Warner Books, 2002).

Brag! The Art of Tooting Your Own Horn Without Blowing It, Peggy Klaus (Warner Books, 2003).

Composing a Life, Mary Catherine Bateson (Plume, 1990).

Difficult Conversations: How to Discuss What Matters Most, Douglas Stone, Bruce Patton, Sheila Heen, and Roger Fisher (Penguin, 2000).

The Drama of the Gifted Child: The Search for the True Self, Alice Miller (Basic Books, 1996).

Essential Managers: Negotiating Skills, Tim Hindle and Robert Heller (DK Publishers, 1999).

Feel the Fear and Beyond: Mastering the Techniques for Doing It Anyway, Susan Jeffers (Random House, 1998).

Feel the Fear and Do It Anyway, Susan Jeffers (Fawcett Books, 1992).

Getting Past No: Negotiating with Difficult People, William Ury (Bantam Doubleday Dell Audio, 1991).

Hardball for Women: Winning at the Game of Business, Pat Heim, Ph.D. (Plume, 1993).

How to Think Like Leonardo DaVinci, Michael Gelb (Dell, 2000).

If My Career's on the Fast Track, Where Do I Get a Road Map?, Anne B. Fisher (William Morrow & Company, 2001).

The Organized Executive: A Program for Productivity, Stephanie Winston (Warner Books, 2001).

Organized to Be Your Best: Simply and Improve How You Work, Susan Silver (Adams Hall Publishers, 2000).

Overcoming Your Strengths: 8 Reasons Why Successful People Derail and How to Remain on Track, Lois P. Frankel, Ph.D. (Harmony, 1997; Corporate Coaching International Publications, 2003).

Power Talk: Using Language to Build Authority and Influence, Sarah Myers McGinty (Warner Books, 2001).

Same Game, Different Rules: How to Get Ahead without Being a Bully Broad, Ice Queen, or "Ms. Understood," Jean Hollands (McGraw-Hill, 2001).

The Secret Handshake: Mastering the Politics of the Business Inner Circle, Kathleen Kelley Reardon (Doubleday, 2002).

The Shadow Negotiation: How Women Can Master the Hidden Agendas That Determine Bargaining Success, Deborah Kolb and Judith Williams (Little, Brown & Company, 2001).

Since Strangling Isn't an Option: Dealing with Difficult People, Common Problems, and Uncommon Solutions, Sandra Crowe (Perigee, 1999).

Talking from 9 to 5: How Women's and Men's Conversational Styles Affect Who Gets Heard, Who Gets Credit, and What Gets Done at Work (Simon & Schuster, 1994).

Talking Money: Everything You Need to Know about Your Finances and Your Future, Jean Chatzky (Warner Books, 2002).

Warming the Stone Child: Myths and Stories about Abandonment and the Unmothered Child, audiotape (Sounds True, 1997).

Why Good Girls Don't Get Ahead . . . But Gutsy Girls Do: 9 Secrets Every Working Woman Must Know, Kate White (Warner Books, 2002).

Women, Anger & Depression: Strategies for Self-Empowerment, Lois P. Frankel, Ph.D. (Health Communications, 1991).

Women's Reality, Anne Wilson Schaef (Harper, 1992).

Women's Ways of Knowing, Mary Field Belenky, Blythe McVicker Clincy, Nancy Rule Goldberger, and Jill Mattuck Tarule (Basic Books, 1986).

Working with Emotional Intelligence, Daniel Goleman (Bantam Doubleday Dell, 2000).

You Are the Message: Getting What You Want By Being Who You Are, Roger Ailes (Currency Doubleday, 1989).

WEB SITES WORTH A VISIT

* http://www.petermontoya.com
Personal Brand magazine is available through this Web site, as is other information about how you can create and market your own personal brand.

* http://www.fortune.com/careers/
This specific site is part of *Fortune* magazine and focuses on career-related issues, including an on-line Ask Annie column.

* http://www.ivillage.com/work/
Using interactive tools, this site presents ideas and feature articles of interest to women, from dieting and divorce to child care and career counseling.

* http://www.advancingwomen.com/workplace.html
This award-winning Web site provides coaching, mentoring, strategy, and support, empowering women to route around traditional choke points in their careers and keep advancing to the highest level of their capabilities.

- http://www.advisorteam.com/user/ksintrol.asp

This site allows you to take and score the Keirsey Temperament Sorter II, an interesting and revealing questionnaire that helps you to decipher your personality style and, in turn, the kind of work you might find most satisfying. It's the same test used in career development programs at *Fortune* 500 companies and in counseling centers and career placement centers at major universities.

About the Author

Lois P. Frankel, Ph.D., is president of Corporate Coaching International. She is an internationally recognized expert in the field of workplace behavior and the empowerment of women. In addition to her work with executives and managers at *Fortune* 100 companies, Dr. Frankel is a sought-after speaker who provides insights and practical tools for increasing career success. A member of the American Psychological Association, National Speakers Association, and Society for Human Resources Management, Dr. Frankel is also a licensed psychotherapist with a doctorate in counseling psychology from the University of Southern California.

Dr. Frankel has been featured in newspapers and magazines, including *Fast Company* and *Entrepreneur*, and quoted extensively as an expert in her field in publications such as *Fortune*, *Working Mother*, the *Los Angeles Times*, and the *Miami Herald*. She is the author of *Overcoming Your Strengths*, which was named by *Fast Company* magazine as "the best unsung business book of the year" in 1997, as well as *Women, Anger, & Depression* and *Kindling the Spirit*.

Dr. Frankel can be reached through either of her Web sites:
www.corporatecoachingintl.com
or
www.gr8speakers.com